Real-Life English

A COMPETENCY–BASED ESL PROGRAM FOR ADULTS

Program Consultants

Jayme Adelson-Goldstein
North Hollywood Learning Center
North Hollywood, California

Julia Collins
Los Angeles Unified School District
El Monte-Rosemead Adult School
El Monte, California

Else V. Hamayan
Illinois Resource Center
Des Plaines, Illinois

Kent Heitman
Carver Community Middle School
Delray Beach, Florida

Patricia De Hesus-Lopez
Texas A & M University
Kingsville, Texas

Federico Salas-Isnardi
Houston Community College
Adult Literacy Programs
Houston, Texas

Connie Villaruel
El Monte-Rosemead Adult School
El Monte, California

Wei-hua (Wendy) Wen
Adult & Continuing Education
New York City Board of Education
New York, New York

STECK-VAUGHN
ELEMENTARY · SECONDARY · ADULT · LIBRARY

A Harcourt Company

www.steck-vaughn.com

◆ ACKNOWLEDGMENTS

Staff Credits:

Executive Editor ◆ Ellen Lehrburger
Senior Editor ◆ Tim Collins
Design Manager ◆ Richard Balsam
Cover Design ◆ Richard Balsam
Photo Editor ◆ Margie Foster

Photo Credits:
Cover: James Minor, Cooke Photographics (title); © Randal Alhadeff–p.13, 86;
© Michelle Bridwell–p.16; © Leslie Bowen–p.129a, 140b; © Jack Demuth–p.97b;
© Patti Gilliam–p.114; © Stephanie Huebinger–p.30, 58, 60; James Minor–p.2, 3, 4, 7;
© Park Street–p.45b, 45c, 45d, 115c, 115d, 123b, 128; © Daniel Thompson
Photography–p.44, 72-74, 78, 88, 97a, 100, 102, 123a, 123c, 124, 129d, 140d;
© Ken Walker–115a, 115b, 129b, 140c; Rick Williams–p.11b, 11c, 12b, 12c, 109, 110;
Sandy Wilson–p.11a, 11d, 11e, 11f, 12a, 12d, 12e, 12f, 31.

Additional Photography by:
P.45a © Gene Lincoln/Tony Stone Worldwide; p.129c, 140a © Peter Vandermark/Stock
Boston.

Illustration Credits:
The Ivy League of Artists, Inc.

Additional Illustration by:
Scott Bieser–p.67, 68, 71, 81a-c, 82a-c, 84a-c, 84f, 94; David Griffin–p.77 (bills);
John Harrison–p.77 (coins); John Hartwell–p.17, 18, 20-22, 24-26, 28;
Jimmy Longacre–p.27; Gary McElhaney–p.9; Lyle Miller–p.89, 98.

Contributing Writer to the First Edition:
Lynne Lilley Robinson
Division of Adult and Continuing Education
Sweetwater Union High School District, Chula Vista, California

Electronic Production:
International Electronic Publishing Center, Inc.

CONTENTS

Units	Competencies	Recognition Words
LITERACY LEVEL		
Introductory Unit	Use left-to-right and top-to-bottom progression Identify, say, and write letters **a** through **z** Identify, say, and write numerals **0** through **90** Discriminate among lower-case letters Discriminate among capital letters Match capital and lower-case letters Read direction lines used throughout the book	listen ◆ look ◆ say ◆ raise your hand ◆ circle ◆ write ◆ underline ◆ work with a partner
Personal Communication	Ask for and give personal information Complete a simple form Introduce oneself	address ◆ city ◆ first name ◆ last name ◆ name ◆ number ◆ state ◆ street ◆ telephone number ◆ zip code
Our Community	Identify places Say where places are Buy stamps and mail letters Understand emergency words Report emergencies by telephone	accident ◆ ambulance ◆ bank ◆ fire ◆ fire department ◆ hospital ◆ mailbox ◆ police station ◆ post office ◆ school ◆ stamp
School and Country	Identify people and places at school Say room numbers Identify classroom objects	board ◆ book ◆ country ◆ desk ◆ library ◆ men's room ◆ office ◆ room ◆ student ◆ teacher ◆ women's room
Daily Living	Ask for, say, and write the time Ask for, say, and write the day of the week Ask for, say, and write the date	date ◆ date of birth ◆ days of the week ◆ month ◆ time ◆ today ◆ tomorrow ◆ year
Food	Identify kinds of food Identify kinds of food packaging Ask where things are in a store Comparison shop	aisle ◆ bag ◆ bottle ◆ box ◆ dairy ◆ food ◆ fruit and vegetables ◆ juice ◆ meat ◆ sale ◆ supermarket ◆ $ ◆ ¢
Shopping	Identify kinds of clothes Ask how much something costs Understand amounts of money Read size tags, price tags, and receipts Write checks Ask to return something	cash ◆ cents ◆ charge ◆ check ◆ dollar ◆ driver's license ◆ ID ◆ receipt ◆ $ ◆ ¢
Home	Say where they live Identify kinds of housing Identify furniture and rooms Read for-rent signs Ask about the rent and the deposit	apartment ◆ bathroom ◆ bed ◆ bedroom ◆ chair ◆ deposit ◆ house ◆ kitchen ◆ lamp ◆ living room ◆ refrigerator ◆ rent ◆ sofa ◆ stove ◆ table
Health Care	Identify parts of the body Describe symptoms and injuries Read medicine labels Make doctors' appointments	arm ◆ capsule ◆ cold ◆ cough ◆ fever ◆ flu ◆ foot ◆ hand ◆ headache ◆ leg ◆ medicine ◆ sick ◆ sore throat ◆ stomach-ache ◆ tablespoon ◆ tablet ◆ teaspoon
Employment	Identify kinds of jobs Give their work experience Give and follow instructions Read help-wanted signs Complete a simple job application	application ◆ days ◆ experience ◆ help wanted ◆ job ◆ nights ◆ pay ◆ weekends
Transportation	Identify kinds of transportation Read traffic signs Ask for schedule and fare information	bicycle ◆ bus ◆ bus stop ◆ car ◆ don't walk ◆ drive ◆ fare ◆ no parking ◆ one way ◆ ride ◆ speed limit ◆ stop ◆ subway ◆ train ◆ walk

LEVEL 1		
Units	**Competencies**	**Grammar**
Personal Communication	Ask for and give personal information Say hello Introduce oneself Complete an identification form	Present tense of **be,** statements Subject pronouns Possessive adjectives Questions with **where + from**
Our Community	Identify places Tell where places are Read maps Ask for, give, and follow directions Use a pay phone to report an emergency	Present tense of **be** **yes/no** questions, short answers Prepositions of location **A/an** Questions with **where**

School and Country	Listen for room numbers
	Identify people and places at school
	Talk about where places are in buildings
	Read building directories
	Write absentee notes
		Present progressive tense
		   statements, negatives, **yes/no**
		   questions, short answers
		Questions with **what** and **where**
		Possessive nouns

Daily Living	Talk about seasons and weather
	Ask for, say, and write times and dates
	Read calendars
	Listen for times and dates
	Listen to weather forecasts
	Read store hour signs
		Expressions with **it**
		   statements, negatives, questions,
		   short answers

Food	Identify kinds of food Write shopping lists Identify food packaging Ask where things are in a supermarket Listen for aisle numbers Read price tags and expiration dates	Singular and plural nouns Mass/count distinction **A/an** or **some** Questions with **how much** and **how many**

Shopping	Identify clothes by article, size, and color
	Shop for clothes
	Write checks
	Read clothing ads and comparison shop
	Listen for and say prices and totals
	Read size tags, price tags, and receipts
		This/that/these/those
		Simple present tense
		   statements, negatives, questions,
		   short answers

Home	Identify rooms, furniture, and housing
	Read for-rent ads
	Ask for utilities to be turned on
	Ask for simple repairs
		There's/there are
		   statements, negatives, questions,
		   short answers
		Prepositions of location

Health Care	Identify kinds of health clinics Read a thermometer Make doctors' appointments Talk about symptoms and injuries Listen to doctors' instructions	Simple present tense of **have** Simple present tense of **feel** Questions with **how**

Employment	Identify kinds of jobs
	Give their work experience and skills
	Read help-wanted ads
	Complete job applications
	Understand safety warnings
		Can, statements, negatives, questions,
		   short answers
		Simple past tense of **be**
		Questions with **how long;** answers with
		   for/from...to

Transportation and Travel	Identify kinds of transportation Read traffic signs Use public transportation Listen for bus numbers and fares	Simple present and present progressive tenses (review and contrast) Questions with **which**

LEVEL 2

Units	Competencies	Grammar
Personal Communication	Identify people in their families Give personal information Introduce people Describe people Apply for a driver's license	Present tense of **be** (review) Simple present tense (review) Present tense of **have** (review) Object pronouns
Our Community	Identify bank services Complete deposit and withdrawal slips Listen for amounts due Buy money orders Buy stamps and send packages	Simple past tense statements, negatives, **wh-** questions Irregular verbs in the simple past tense
Our Country	Identify branches of government Identify citizenship requirements Complete a citizenship application Describe the U.S. flag Say the Pledge of Allegiance	Contrast of simple present and present progressive tenses (review) **Have to** **(I)'d like to**

Daily Living	Describe their native countries
	Talk about why they came to the U.S.
	Describe how they felt when they came
	   to the U.S.
	Talk about where they have lived
		Simple past tense
		   wh- questions, **yes/no** questions,
		   short answers
		More irregular verbs in the simple past
		   tense

Food	Read recipes and package directions Listen to supermarket ads Read supermarket ads Identify sales and coupons	**Some** and **any** statements, negatives, questions Imperatives
Shopping	Comparison shop Identify forms of payment Ask for refunds and exchanges Identify sales tax Read clothing care labels	Comparative adjectives with **-er** and **more**
Home	Talk about housing and neighborhoods Read for-rent ads Complete a change of address form Read utility bills	Adverbials of location Questions and short answers with **there**
Health Care	Identify kinds of doctors Talk about symptoms and medicine Identify practices that lead to good health Complete medical history forms Listen to doctors' advice Read medicine labels	**Should/shouldn't** Conditional sentences with **should** or with imperatives
Employment	Ask about job openings Interview for a job ♦ Accept a job offer Complete a Social Security form Listen to instructions at work Explain absences from work	Polite requests with **could** Clauses with **so** and **because**
Transportation and Travel	Talk about getting a driver's license Identify safe driving practices Identify car maintenance procedures Ask for and give road directions Read road maps	**Should/shouldn't** (review) **Have to** (review) Conditional sentences with **should** or with imperatives (review) Clauses with **so** and **because** (review)

LEVEL 3

Units	Competencies	Grammar
Personal Communication	Identify recreational activities Listen to taped announcements Interpret recreational schedules Complete registration forms	**And/or/but** Gerunds and infinitives
Our Community	Report utility problems Use the telephone directory Identify community service agencies Leave and take telephone messages Check telephone bills	Object pronouns with **for** and **to** **Should/shouldn't** (review)
Our Country	Read weather maps Understand U.S. geography Read weather reports Listen to weather reports	Expressions with **it** (review) Future with **going to** Adverbs with **-ly**
Daily Living	Identify community issues Identify community groups Write to elected officials Interpret cost-of-living charts	Present perfect tense with **for** and **since** statements, negatives, **yes/no** questions, short answers Irregular past participles Reporting speech in the present tense
Food	Read menus Order in restaurants Talk about food preferences Identify the basic food groups	Linking verbs Comparative adjectives with **-er** and **more** (review) Superlative adjectives with **-est** and **most**
Shopping	Identify kinds of stores Read a catalog Order by mail Identify clothes by article, size, and material	Nouns used as adjectives Sequence of modification
Home	Talk about household maintenance Understand home safety precautions Ask for household repairs Read public service ads Read product labels	Clauses with **when/while** and the simple past/past progressive tenses Clauses with **before/after** and the simple past tense **Make/do**
Health Care	Report accidents Call the poison control center Listen to first-aid instructions Read first-aid product packages Understand first-aid procedures	Reflexive pronouns Conditional sentences with **will**
Employment	Report whether work is complete Identify work safety equipment Listen to safety instructions at work Read notices at work Check paychecks	Simple past tense with **ago** Present perfect tense with **already** and **yet**
Transportation and Travel	Make travel plans and buy tickets Identify kinds of transportation Listen to travel announcements Check travel tickets	Future with **going to** (review) Conditional sentences with **will** (review) Present perfect tense with **ever/never**

LEVEL 4		
Units	**Competencies**	**Grammar**
Personal Communication	Offer invitations Accept invitations Turn down invitations Write invitations	Present tenses (review) present tense of **be**, simple present, present progressive **Feel** (review)
Our Community	Endorse checks Pay by check Compare bank services Balance checkbooks	Past tenses (review) simple past, past progressive Clauses with **when** and **while** **Used to** statements, questions
Our Country	Read about U.S. history Understand the U.S. Constitution Understand equal educational opportunity	Simple past tense with **ago** (review) Present perfect tense with **for** and **since**
Daily Living	Identify environmental problems Identify community problems Read about environmental solutions	Passive voice (simple present, simple past) Gerunds and infinitives as objects
Food	Identify kinds of stores Understand unit cost Read ingredients on food packages	Gerunds as objects of prepositions **It's** + adjective + infinitive
Shopping	Identify kinds of stores Read garage sale ads Write garage sale ads Read warranties	**Wh-** questions (review) Restrictive relative clauses
Home	Correct household hazards Request repairs Write complaint letters Read leases	**Must/may** Gerunds as subjects Conditional sentences with **could**
Health Care	Identify good health habits Answer a doctor's questions Compare and choose insurance plans Complete insurance claim forms	**Must be** (possibility) **Should/ought to/had better** (advice)
Employment	Talk about education, work experience, and career plans Identify traits of good employees Talk about rules at work Identify job benefits	Gerunds as subjects and objects (review) Present and past participles
Transportation and Travel	Understand car maintenance and repair Identify safe driving practices Complete customer complaint forms Read auto product labels	Present perfect tense (review)

Real-Life English is a complete competency-based, four-skill program for teaching ESL to adults and young adults. The program is designed for students enrolled in public or private schools, in learning centers, or in institutes, or for individuals working with tutors. *Real-Life English* consists of four levels plus a Literacy Level for use prior to or together with Level 1.

◆ FEATURES

◆ *Real-Life English* **is competency-based.** *Real-Life English's* competency-based syllabus gives adult students the life skills they need to succeed in the U.S. The syllabus is compatible with the CASAS Competencies, the Mainstream English Language Training Project (MELT and the BEST Test), and with state curriculums for adult ESL from Texas and California.

The *About You* symbol appears on the Student Book page each time students use a competency. These activities are always personalized and communicative or life-skill based.

◆ *Real-Life English* **is communicative.** Numerous conversational models and communicative activities—including mixers, problem-solving activities, and information-gap activities—get students talking from the start.

◆ *Real-Life English* **addresses all four language skills.** Listening, speaking, reading, and writing are developed in separate sections in each unit. In addition, competency-based Word Bank and Structure Base sections in each unit develop the vocabulary and grammar students need.

◆ *Real-Life English* **is appropriate for adults.** The language and situations presented in *Real-Life English* are ones adults are likely to encounter in the U.S. The abundance of attractive, true-to-life photographs, illustrations, and realia will interest and motivate adults.

◆ *Real-Life English* **starts at the appropriate level for beginning students.** The Literacy Level is designed for students who have no prior knowledge of English and have few or no literacy skills in their native language(s) or are literate in a language with a non-Roman alphabet. Level 1 is intended for students with little or no prior knowledge of English. As students continue through the program, they reach progressively higher levels of language and life-skills. For information on placement, see page vi of the Introduction to the Student Book.

♦ *Real-Life English* **is appropriate for multi-level classes.** Because unit topics carry over from level to level, the series is ideal for use in multi-level classes. Units are situational and non-sequential, making *Real-Life English* appropriate for open-entry/open-exit situations.

COMPONENTS

Real-Life English consists of:

- ♦ Five Student Books (Literacy and Levels 1–4)

- ♦ Four Workbooks (Levels 1–4)

- ♦ Five Teacher's Editions (Literacy and Levels 1–4)

- ♦ Audiocassettes (Literacy and Levels 1–4)

Student Books

Each two-color Student Book consists of ten fourteen-page units. (Units are twelve pages each in the Literacy Level.) Each unit is organized around a single competency-based topic, providing students with ample time on task to acquire the target competencies and language.

♦ **For easy teaching and learning, the Student Books follow a consistent format.** Each book has ten consistently organized units, each of which can be taught in approximately six to ten classroom sessions. In addition, each unit follows a consistent pattern. For more information, see page iv of the Introduction to the Student Book.

♦ **A separate Literacy Level Student Book builds literacy and life skills.** Students learn foundation literacy skills in tandem with listening and speaking skills. The competency-based syllabus ensures that students get the life skills they need to live in the U.S.

♦ **Clear directions, abundant examples, and pedagogical use of color assure that students always know exactly what**

to do. Boldface type is used in direction lines to make them easy for students to find and read. Exercise examples make tasks clear to students and teachers. To facilitate personalization, color is used in dialogs and exercises to indicate words that students are to change when they are talking or writing about themselves.

♦ **Check Your Competency pages provide a complete evaluation program.** Teachers can use these pages to evaluate students' progress and to track the program's learner verification needs. Success is built in because competencies are always checked in familiar formats.

Workbooks

The Workbooks for Levels 1–4 contain ten eight-page units plus a complete Answer Key at the back of each book. Each Workbook unit contains at least one exercise for each section of the Student Book. To allow for additional reinforcement of vocabulary and structure, there are multiple exercises for Word Bank and Structure Base.

Teacher's Editions

The complete Teacher's Editions help both new and experienced teachers organize their teaching, motivate their students, and successfully use a variety of individual, pair, and group activities.

♦ **Unit Overviews provide valuable information on how to motivate students and organize teaching.** Each Unit Overview contains an optional Unit Warm-Up teachers can use to build students' interest and get them ready for the unit. Each opener also contains a list of optional materials— including pictures, flash cards, and realia—teachers can use to enliven instruction throughout the entire unit.

♦ **The Teacher's Editions contain complete suggested procedures for every part of the Student Book.** Each section of a unit begins with a list of the competencies developed on the Student Book page(s). Teachers can use this list when planning lessons. Then teaching notes give suggestions for a recommended three-part lesson format:

Preparation: Suggestions for preteaching the new language, competencies, and concepts on the Student Book page(s).

Presentation: Suggested procedures for working with the Student Book page(s) in class.

Follow-Up: A suggested optional activity teachers can use to provide additional reinforcement or to enrich and extend the new language and competencies. The Follow-Ups include a variety of interactive pair and small group activities, as well as numerous reading and writing activities. Each activity has a suggested variant, marked with ♦, for use with students who require activities at a slightly more sophisticated level. For teaching ease, the corresponding Workbook exercise(s) for each page or section of the Student Book are indicated on the Teacher's Edition page.

♦ **The Teacher's Editions contain numerous Teaching Notes, Culture Notes, and Language Notes.** Teachers can share this wealth of information with students or use it in lesson planning.

♦ **Each Teacher's Edition unit concludes with English in Action, an optional holistic cooperative learning project.** Students will find these to be valuable and stimulating culminating activities.

♦ **Additional features.** A Listening Transcript is in each Teacher's Edition. The Teacher's Editions also contain Individual Competency Charts for each unit and a Class Cumulative Competency Chart for teachers to record students' progress and to track the program's learner verification needs.

Audiocassettes

▭▭ The Audiocassettes at each level contain all dialogs and listening activities marked with this cassette symbol in the Student Book. The Audiocassettes give students experience in listening to a variety of native speakers in authentic situations. The Listening Transcript in each Student Book and Teacher's Edition contains scripts for all listening selections not appearing directly on the pages of the Student Books.

Real-Life English

A COMPETENCY–BASED ESL PROGRAM FOR ADULTS

Program Consultants

Jayme Adelson-Goldstein
North Hollywood Learning Center
North Hollywood, California

Julia Collins
Los Angeles Unified School District
El Monte-Rosemead Adult School
El Monte, California

Else V. Hamayan
Illinois Resource Center
Des Plaines, Illinois

Kent Heitman
Carver Community Middle School
Delray Beach, Florida

Patricia De Hesus-Lopez
Texas A & M University
Kingsville, Texas

Federico Salas-Isnardi
Houston Community College
Adult Literacy Programs
Houston, Texas

Connie Villaruel
El Monte-Rosemead Adult School
El Monte, California

Wei-hua (Wendy) Wen
Adult & Continuing Education
New York City Board of Education
New York, New York

STECK-VAUGHN
COMPANY
A Subsidiary of National Education Corporation

Real-Life English is a complete competency-based, four-skill program for teaching ESL to adults and young adults. *Real-Life English* follows a competency-based syllabus that is compatible with the CASAS and MELT (BEST Test) competencies, as well as state curriculums for competency-based adult ESL from Texas and California.

Real-Life English is designed for students enrolled in public or private schools, in learning centers, or in institutes, and for individuals working with tutors. The program consists of four levels plus a Literacy Level for use prior to or together with Level 1. *Real-Life English* has these components:

◆ Five Student Books (Literacy and Levels 1–4).

◆ Five Teacher's Editions (Literacy and Levels 1–4), which provide detailed suggestions on how to present each section of the Student Book in class.

◆ Four Workbooks (Levels 1–4), which provide reinforcement for each section of the Student Books.

◆ Audiocassettes (Literacy and Levels 1–4), which contain all dialogs and listening activities in the Student Books. This symbol on the Student Book page indicates each time material for that page is on the Audiocassettes. A transcript of all material recorded on the tapes but not appearing directly on the Student Book pages is at the back of each Student Book and Teacher's Edition.

Each level consists of ten units. Because the unit topics carry over from level to level, *Real-Life English* is ideal for multi-level classes.

The *About You* symbol, a unique feature, appears on the Student Book page each time students use a competency. To facilitate personalization, color is used in dialogs and exercises. After students have learned a dialog or completed an exercise, they can easily adapt it to talk or write about themselves by changing the words in color.

Organization of Student Book 1

Each unit contains these eleven sections:

Unit Opener

Each Unit Opener includes a list of unit competencies, a photo and accompanying questions, and a chant. (In Levels 2–4, dialogs, short articles, and brief narrative stories appear in place of chants.) Teachers can use the list of competencies for their own reference, or they can have students read it so that they, too, are aware of the unit's goals. The photo and questions activate students' prior knowledge by getting them to think and talk about the unit topic. The chants provide an exciting start to every unit. Chants are also an excellent means of developing accurate pronunciation, intonation, and stress. For more information, see "Presenting Chants" on page vi.

Starting Out

Starting Out presents most of the new competencies, concepts, and language in the unit. It generally consists of a dialog or captioned pictures, questions, and an *About You* activity.

Talk It Over

Talk It Over introduces additional competencies, language, and concepts, usually in the form of a dialog. The dialog becomes the model for an interactive *About You* activity.

Word Bank

Word Bank presents and develops vocabulary. The first part of the page contains a list of the new key words and phrases grouped by category. The Useful Language box contains common expressions, clarification strategies, and idioms students use in the unit. Oral and written exercises and *About You* activities provide purposeful and communicative reinforcement of the new vocabulary.

Listening

The Listening page develops competency-based listening comprehension skills. Tasks include listening for addresses, telephone numbers, prices, directions, and doctors' instructions.

All the activities develop the skill of **focused listening.** Students learn to recognize the information they need and to listen selectively for only that information. They do not have to understand every word; rather, they have to filter out everything except the information they want to find out. This essential skill is used by native speakers of all languages.

Many of the activities involve **multi-task listening.** Students listen to the same selection several times and complete a different task each time. First they might listen for the main idea. They might listen again for specific information. They might listen a third time in order to draw conclusions or make inferences.

Culminating discussion questions allow students to relate the information they have heard to their own needs and interests.

Reading

The selections in Reading, such as help-wanted ads, store receipts, supermarket ads, and food packages, focus on life-skill based tasks. Exercises, discussion questions, and *About You* activities develop reading skills and help students relate the content of the selections to their lives.

Structure Base

Structure Base, a two-page spread, presents key grammatical structures that complement the unit competencies. Language boxes show the new language in a clear, simple format that allows students to make generalizations about the new language. Oral and written exercises provide contextualized reinforcement of each new grammar point.

Writing

On the Writing page students develop authentic writing skills, such as completing job applications, writing absentee notes to children's teachers, and writing checks.

One To One

Each One To One section presents a competency-based information-gap activity. Students are presented with incomplete or partial information that they must complete by finding out the missing information from their partners. Topics include giving directions, reading rental ads, and comparing sales at two stores. In many units, culminating discussion questions encourage students to relate the information they gathered to their own needs and interests.

Extension

The Extension page enriches the previous instruction with activities at a slightly more advanced level. As in other sections, realia is used extensively. Oral and written exercises and *About You* activities help students master the competencies, language, and concepts, and relate them to their lives.

Check Your Competency

The Check Your Competency pages are designed to allow teachers to track students' progress and to meet schools' or programs' learner verification needs. All competencies are tested in the same manner they are presented in the units, so formats are familiar and non-threatening, and success is built in. The list of competencies at the top of the page alerts teachers and students to the competencies that are being evaluated. The check-off boxes allow students to track their success and gain a sense of accomplishment and satisfaction.

 This *Check Up* symbol on the Check Your Competency pages denotes when a competency is evaluated. For more information on this section, see "Evaluation" on page viii.

Placement

Any number of tests can be used to place students in the appropriate level of *Real-Life English*. The following tables indicate placement based on the CASAS and MELT (BEST Test) standards.

Student Performance Levels	CASAS Achievement Score	Real-Life English
	164 or under	Literacy
I	165–185	Level 1
II	186–190	
III	191–196	Level 2
IV	197–205	
V	206–210	Level 3
VI	211–216	
VII	217–225	Level 4
VIII	226 (+)	

Teaching Techniques

Presenting Chants

The chants can be used in a variety of ways. Students can learn to say the chants aloud, or they can listen to and/or read the chants and then answer questions about them. All the chants are recorded on the Audiocassettes. To present a chant, we suggest these steps:

♦ Play the tape or say the chant aloud one or two times as students listen. Establish a firm, steady beat by tapping your foot, clapping your hands, or snapping your fingers. Ask a few questions to make sure students understand. Clarify any words students need to know.

♦ Teach students the chant line-by-line. Say each line and have the class repeat chorally.

♦ Have the class say or read the chant chorally

while you take one of the parts.

♦ Divide the class into as many groups as there are parts in the chant, and have the groups say or read it chorally.

A number of techniques can be used to lend variety and excitement to the chants:

♦ Students might clap or tap out the rhythm as they say the chant. This will make the chant livelier and help students hear the rhythm better.

♦ Two or three students might act out the chant in front of the class as the rest of the class reads or says the chant.

♦ You might bring in (or have students bring in) simple props, costumes, and rhythm instruments.

Feel free to have the class say the chant throughout the rest of the unit. Students might enjoy saying the chant as a quick warm-up at the start of each class session.

Presenting Dialogs

To present a dialog, follow these suggested steps:

♦ Play the tape or say the dialog aloud two or more times. Ask one or two simple questions to make sure students understand.

♦ Say the dialog aloud line-by-line for students to repeat chorally, by rows, and then individually.

♦ Have students say or read the dialog together in pairs.

♦ Have several pairs say or read the dialog aloud for the class.

Reinforcing Vocabulary

To reinforce the words in the list on the Word Bank page, have students look over the list. Clarify any words they do not recognize. To provide additional reinforcement, use any of these techniques:

- **Vocabulary notebooks.** Have students use each new word to say a sentence for you to write on the board. Have students copy all of the sentences into their vocabulary notebooks.

- **Personal dictionaries.** Students can start personal dictionaries. For each new word students can write a simple definition and/or draw or glue in a picture of the object or the action.

- **Flash cards.** Flash cards are easy for you or for students to make. Write a new word or phrase on the front of each card. Provide a simple definition or a picture of the object or action on the back of the card. Students can use the cards to review vocabulary or to play a variety of games, such as Concentration.

- **The Remember-It Game.** Use this simple memory game to review vocabulary of every topic. For example, to reinforce food words, start the game by saying, *We're having a picnic, and we're going to bring apples.* The next student has to repeat the list and add an item. If someone cannot remember the whole list or cannot add a word, he or she has to drop out. The student who can remember the longest list wins.

Presenting Listening Activities

Use any of these suggestions:

- To activate students' prior knowledge, have them look at the illustrations, if any, and say as much as they can about them. Encourage them to make inferences about the content of the listening selection.

- Have students read the directions. To encourage them to focus their listening, have them read the questions so that they know exactly what to listen for.

- Play the tape or read the Listening Transcript aloud as students complete the activity. Rewind the tape and play it again as necessary.

- Check students' work.

In multi-task listenings, remind students that they will listen to the same passage several times and answer different questions each time. After students complete a section, check their work (or have students check their own or each others' work) before you rewind the tape and proceed to the next questions.

Prereading

To help students read the selections with ease and success, establish a purpose for reading and call on students' prior knowledge to make inferences about the reading. Use any of these techniques:

- Have students look over and describe any photographs, realia, and/or illustrations. Ask them to use the illustrations to say what they think the selection might be about.

- Have students read the title and any heads or sub-heads. Ask them what kind of information they think is in the selection and how it might be organized. Ask them where they might encounter such information outside of class and why they would want to read it.

- Have students read the questions that follow the selection to help them focus their reading. Ask them what kind of information they think they will find out when they read. Restate their ideas and/or write them on the board in acceptable English.

- Remind students that they do not have to know all the words in order to understand the selection. Then have students complete the activities on the page. Check their answers.

One To One

To use these information gap activities to maximum advantage, follow these steps:

- Put students in pairs, assign the roles of A and B, and have students turn to the appropriate pages. Make sure that students look only at their assigned pages.

- Present the dialog in Step 1. Follow the instructions in "Presenting Dialogs" on page vi. (Please note that as these conversations are intended to be models for free conversation, they are not recorded on the Audiocassettes.)

- When students can say the dialog with confidence, model Step 2 with a student. Remind students that they need to change the words in color to adapt the dialog in 1 to each new situation. Then have students complete the activity.

- Have students continue with the remaining steps on the page. For additional practice, make sure students switch roles (Student A becomes Student B and vice versa) and repeat Steps 2 and 3. When all students have completed all parts of both pages, check everyone's work, or have students check their own or each others' work.

Evaluation

To use the Check Your Competency pages successfully, follow these suggested procedures.

Before and during each evaluation, create a relaxed, affirming atmosphere. Chat with the students for a few minutes and review the material. When you and the students are ready, have students read the directions and look over each exercise before they complete it. If at any time you sense that students are becoming frustrated, stop to provide additional review. Resume when students are ready. The evaluation formats follow two basic patterns:

1. Speaking competencies are checked in the same two-part format used to present them in the unit. In the first part, a review, students fill in missing words in a brief conversation. In the second part, marked with the *Check Up* symbol, students' ability to use the competency is checked. Students use the dialog they have just completed as a model for their own conversations. As in the rest of the unit, color

indicates the words students change to talk about themselves. Follow these suggestions:

- When students are ready, have them complete the written portion. Check their answers. Then have students practice the dialog in pairs.

- Continue with the spoken part of the evaluation. Make sure that students remember that they are to substitute words about themselves for the words in color. Have students complete the spoken part in any or all of these ways:

Self- and Peer Evaluation: Have students complete the spoken activity in pairs. Students in each pair evaluate themselves and/or each other and report the results to you.

Teacher/Pair Evaluation: Have pairs complete the activity as you observe. Begin with the most proficient students. As other students who are ready to be evaluated wait, have them practice in pairs. Students who complete the evaluation successfully can peer-teach those who are waiting or those who need additional review.

Teacher/Individual Evaluation: Have individuals complete the activity with you as partner. Follow the procedures in Teacher/Pair Evaluation.

2. Listening, reading, and **writing** competencies are checked in a simple one-step process. When students are ready to begin, have them read the instructions. Demonstrate the first item and have students complete the activity. Then check their work. If necessary, provide any review needed, and have students try the activity again.

When students demonstrate mastery of a competency to your satisfaction, have them record their success by checking the appropriate box at the top of the Student Book page. The Teacher's Edition also contains charts for you to reproduce and use to keep track of individual and class progress.

Real-Life English

Unit 1 Overview

UNIT WARM-UP

The focus of Unit 1, "Personal Communication," is greetings, introductions, asking for and giving personal information, and completing simple forms. To stimulate a discussion, show them pictures of people greeting each other. Ask students to say words and phrases used to greet people in English.

Teaching Note

Throughout this unit, make a point of greeting the class at the start of each lesson. A warm **Good morning** or **Hello** will create a positive classroom environment and reinforce the content of the unit.

Unit 1 Optional Materials

● A large world map and flags or pins to mark students' countries.

● Personal identification information (a driver's license, a Social Security card, a letter mailed to you at home or at school).

● Overhead transparencies or other examples of the kinds of forms in the unit.

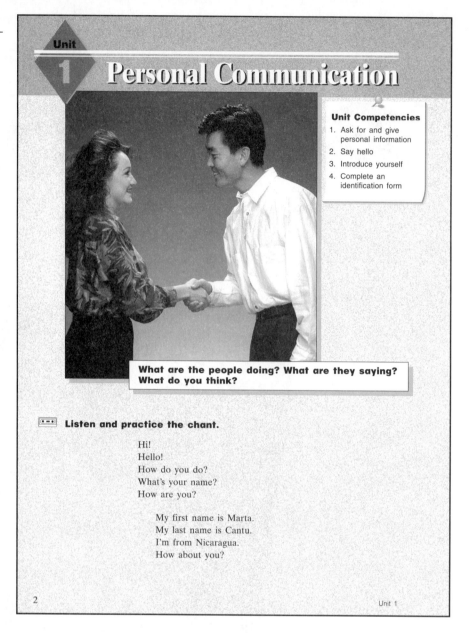

Unit 1

Personal Communication

Unit Competencies
1. Ask for and give personal information
2. Say hello
3. Introduce yourself
4. Complete an identification form

What are the people doing? What are they saying? What do you think?

Listen and practice the chant.

Hi!
Hello!
How do you do?
What's your name?
How are you?

My first name is Marta.
My last name is Cantu.
I'm from Nicaragua.
How about you?

2   Unit 1

COMPETENCIES (page 2)

Ask for and give personal information

Say hello

Introduce themselves

PREPARATION

Use the photograph on the page, pantomime, and the world map to preteach the new language in the chant. Follow these suggestions.

● Tell students your full name, your home country, and the languages you speak. Then put a marker on the map to represent your home country. Have students give the same information about themselves. Help them put markers on the map to indicate their home countries.

● Use the photograph and pantomime to show how English speakers greet. Model the greetings and have students repeat.

Culture Note: Encourage students to make eye contact when greeting. Show them how to take your hand firmly when shaking it. Then have students shake hands with each other.

PRESENTATION

Focus attention on the photo and have students answer the questions. Encourage them to say everything they can about it. Write their ideas on the board or restate them in acceptable English.

Present the chant. See "Presenting Chants" on page vi.

WORKBOOK

Unit 1, Page 1, Exercise 1.

FOLLOW-UP

Different Greetings: Ask students to greet each other in pairs. Have them switch partners several times and repeat.

♦ Have pairs write short lists of greetings. Have them read their lists to the class.

Starting Out

 A. Practice the dialog.

- ➤ Where are you from, **Mei?**
- ● I'm from **China.** I'm **Chinese.**
- ➤ What language do you speak?
- ● I speak **Chinese.**
- ➤ Where do you live?
- ● **San Francisco, California.** How about you?

B. Complete the sentences. Write about yourself.

1. I'm from _____ Answers will vary. _____.
   (country)

2. I'm _____.
   (nationality)

3. I speak _____.
   (language)

4. I live in _____.
   (city, state)

About You **C. Work with a partner.**
Use the dialog in A to talk about yourself.

Unit 1   3

PREPARATION

Tell students your home country, your first/native language, and the city and state where you live. Have students tell you the same information about themselves.

PRESENTATION

A. Have students talk about the photograph. Encourage them to say everything they can about it. Write their ideas on the board or restate them in acceptable English. Then present the dialog. See "Presenting Dialogs" on page vi.

B. Demonstrate by completing the sentence with information about yourself on the board. Then have students complete the activity independently. Ask several students to

read their answers aloud.

Teaching Note: You may want to remind students that the names of countries, states, cities, streets, and languages are capitalized.

About You **C.** Demonstrate by having a student ask you the questions in A. Have students complete the activity. Then have students switch partners and repeat the activity. Ask several pairs of students to present their conversations to the class.

WORKBOOK

Unit 1, Page 1, Exercise 2.

FOLLOW-UP

Questions and Answers: Have small groups of students ask and answer

questions about their home countries, first languages, and the city (cities) and state where they live now. Have group members share what they learned about the other people in their group with the rest of the class.

♦ Have students write the questions and give them to others to answer in writing. Have volunteers tell about other members of the class by reading the written answers they received.

Unit 1   3

Ask for and give personal
    information

Say hello

Introduce themselves

Talk It Over

 A. Practice the dialog.

➤ Hi. I'm a new student in your class.

● Hello. My name's **Ana Smith.** What's your name?

➤ **Pablo Bueno.**

● How do you spell that?

➤ My first name is **Pablo**, P-A-B-L-O. My last name is **Bueno**, B-U-E-N-O.

● Where are you from, **Pablo?**

➤ **Mexico.** I'm **Mexican.**

● What language do you speak?

➤ I speak **Spanish.**

● Nice to meet you, **Pablo.**

➤ Nice to meet you, too, **Ms. Smith.**

**B. Talk to three students.
Use the dialog in A.
Write the answers.**

	First Name	Last Name	Country	Nationality	Language
Example	Pablo	Bueno	Mexico	Mexican	Spanish
Student 1		Answers	will vary.		
Student 2					
Student 3					

PREPARATION

Preteach the new expressions for this dialog: **How do you spell that? Nice to meet you.**

● Help students verify the spelling of their names by having them spell their names aloud while you write them on the board.

Teaching Note: You may want to explain that English speakers use the clarification strategy of asking people to spell their names aloud to find out how to write unfamiliar names.

PRESENTATION

A. Have students talk about the photograph. Encourage them to say everything they can about it. Write their ideas on the board or restate them in acceptable English. Then present the dialog. See "Presenting Dialogs" on page vi.

B. Demonstrate by having a student ask you questions in A. Have students complete the chart by moving about the room, asking each other questions, and writing the answers in their books. Remind students to capitalize people's names and the names of countries, nationalities, and languages. Ask several pairs of students to present their conversations to the class.

WORKBOOK

Unit 1, Page 2, Exercise 3.

FOLLOW–UP

Role-Play: Have pairs of students role-play the first day of class with one playing the teacher and the other playing the new student. Have several pairs of students present their conversations to the class.

◆ Have students write their conversations.

Word Bank

A. Study the vocabulary.

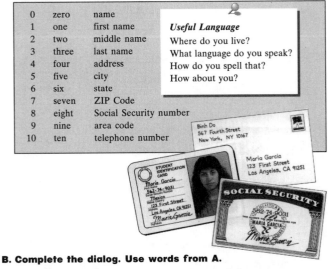

0	zero	name
1	one	first name
2	two	middle name
3	three	last name
4	four	address
5	five	city
6	six	state
7	seven	ZIP Code
8	eight	Social Security number
9	nine	area code
10	ten	telephone number

Useful Language
Where do you live?
What language do you speak?
How do you spell that?
How about you?

B. Complete the dialog. Use words from A.

➤ What's your _____address_____?
● 123 First Street.

➤ What _____city_____ and state do you live in?
● Los Angeles, California.

➤ What's your ZIP _____Code_____?
● 91251.

➤ What's your telephone number, _____area_____ code first?
● (818) 230-2143.

➤ What _____language_____ do you speak?
● Spanish.

 C. Work with a partner
Use the dialog in B to talk about yourself.

Unit 1   5

PREPARATION

Preteach or review the new vocabulary before students open their books. Give special attention to the numbers **zero** through **ten** and the words **middle name, address, ZIP Code, Social Security number, area code,** and **telephone number.** Show students a driver's license, Social Security card, and an envelope addressed to you. Provide any reinforcement necessary. See "Reinforcing Vocabulary" on page vi.

PRESENTATION

A. Have students scan the list. Define, or have other students define, any words individuals do not recognize. Provide any reinforcement necessary. See "Reinforcing Vocabulary" on page vi. Remind students that they can use this list throughout the unit to look up words, to check spelling, and to find key phrases.

B. Demonstrate by doing the first item on the board. Make sure students understand that they should use words from A to complete the exercise. Have students complete the activity independently. Have students say their answers aloud while the other students check their own answers.

C. Demonstrate by having a student ask you the questions in B. Have students complete the activity in pairs. Then have students switch partners and repeat the activi-

ty. Ask several pairs to present their conversations to the class.

WORKBOOK

Unit 1, Pages 2–3, Exercises 4A–4D.

FOLLOW–UP

Phone Book Quiz: Give pairs of students pages from a phone book. Have them imagine that the names listed are their own. Have them ask and answer questions about addresses and phone numbers. Have pairs of students present their conversations to the class.

♦ Have students write the questions they asked in the previous activity. Have them exchange papers and answer each other's questions in writing.

Unit 1   5

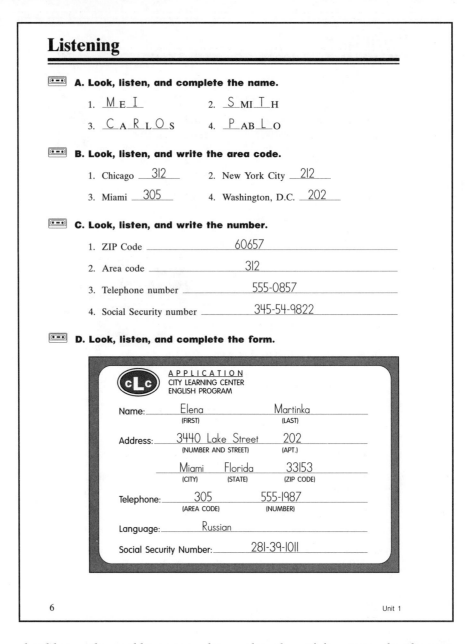

Listening

A. Look, listen, and complete the name.

1. M E I
2. S M I T H
3. C A R L O S
4. P A B L O

B. Look, listen, and write the area code.

1. Chicago ___312___
2. New York City ___212___
3. Miami ___305___
4. Washington, D.C. ___202___

C. Look, listen, and write the number.

1. ZIP Code ___60657___
2. Area code ___312___
3. Telephone number ___555-0857___
4. Social Security number ___345-54-9822___

D. Look, listen, and complete the form.

> **cLc** APPLICATION
> CITY LEARNING CENTER
> ENGLISH PROGRAM
>
> Name: ___Elena___ ___Martinka___
> (FIRST)   (LAST)
>
> Address: ___3440 Lake Street___ ___202___
> (NUMBER AND STREET)   (APT.)
>
> ___Miami___ ___Florida___ ___33153___
> (CITY)   (STATE)   (ZIP CODE)
>
> Telephone: ___305___ ___555-1987___
> (AREA CODE)   (NUMBER)
>
> Language: ___Russian___
>
> Social Security Number: ___281-39-1011___

6

Unit 1

PREPARATION

If necessary, review the new vocabulary. Have students spell their names for each other and exchange ZIP Codes, area codes, telephone numbers, and Social Security numbers. Tell students they should give fictitious information if they would rather not use personal information.

Culture Note: If students do not know what a Social Security number is, explain that all people must have one to keep track of work records and for tax identification. The government uses this number to keep track of taxes paid by each worker and to provide payments when the worker retires. You may want to explain that each person has a personal Social Security number which should never be used by anyone else.

PRESENTATION

A, B, and **C.** Have students complete the activity as you play the tape or read the Listening Transcript aloud two or more times. Check students' work.

Teaching Note: Clarify that all the numbers in this unit are usually said in single digits. Telephone numbers are usually said in single digits with pauses in three places: *3–7–5, 2–3, 4–5.* People often say the letter *o* instead of the number *zero,* as in area code 408 *(four-oh-eight).*

D. Use the board or an overhead projector to present the form in D. Demonstrate how the form is to be filled out. Then have students complete the activity as you play the tape or read the Listening Transcript aloud two or more times. Check students' work.

WORKBOOK

Unit 1, Page 4, Exercise 5.

FOLLOW-UP

Dictation: Spell aloud the words **name, address, city, state,** and **telephone number** for students to write on sheets of paper. Check students' work.

♦ Have students work in pairs. One partner dictates the spelling of a name or gives an address or a phone number while the other partner writes what he or she hears. Then the speaker checks what the listener has written.

Reading

A. Look and read.

CITY LEARNING CENTER BULLETIN
New Students

Pedro Mendoza and Sylvia Li are new students in Level 1.
Pedro Mendoza lives in Miami, Florida.
He's from Puerto Rico.
His address is 820 School Street.
His ZIP Code is 33152.

Sylvia Li is from China.
She lives in Miami, Florida, too.
Her address is 345 Green Street.
Her ZIP Code is 33187.

B. Answer the questions about Pedro and Sylvia.

  _e_ 1. What's his ZIP Code?   a. Li

  _a_ 2. What's her last name?   b. Mendoza

  _d_ 3. Where do they live?   c. 345 Green Street

  _b_ 4. What's his last name?   d. Miami, Florida

  _c_ 5. What's her address?   ✔ e. 33152

C. Complete the sentences about Pedro and Sylvia.

1. Pedro and Sylvia live in _____ Miami, Florida _____.

2. His _____ address _____ is 820 School Street.

3. Her ZIP Code is _____ 33187 _____.

4. _____ Miami _____ is a city in Florida.

Unit 1   7

PREPARATION

If necessary, review the new vocabulary. Follow the instructions in "Preparation" on page 6. You may want to explain the word **bulletin.** Display a newspaper and tell students that a bulletin is a kind of newspaper.

Teaching Note: Students may notice that the two Miami ZIP Codes are different. Explain that large cities are often divided into more than one zone.

PRESENTATION

A. Have students preview the bulletin before they read it. See "Prereading" on page vii. Encourage them to say everything they can about the bulletin. Write their ideas on the board or restate them in acceptable English. Then have them read the bulletin independently.

B. Have students read and answer the questions orally and/or in writing. Have pairs of students compare their answers. Then check everyone's work.

C. Have students read and complete the activity independently. Check students' work.

WORKBOOK

Unit 1, Page 4, Exercise 6.

FOLLOW-UP

News Bulletins: Have students work in small groups to interview each other and create news bulletins, one for each member of the group. Put the bulletins around the room.

♦ Have students interview members of the community, school staff, etc. Then ask students to create bulletins about the people they interview and share them with the class.

Ask for and give personal
information

Introduce themselves

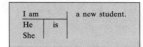

Structure Base

A. Study the examples.

I am		a new student.
He	is	
She		

We		are new students.
You	
They	

B. Complete the sentences. Use the words from A.

1. Tuyet is my friend. ____She is____ from Vietnam.

2. I am Tron. ____I am____ from Vietnam, too.

3. Tuyet and I are in Level 1. ____We are____ new students.

4. Chen and Jiang are in the class, too. ____They are____ from China.

5. Pablo is a new student. ____He is____ from Mexico.

 C. Work with a partner.
Use the sentences in B to talk about the students in
your class.

D. Study the examples.

I	+	am	=	I'm
he	+	is	=	he's
she	+	is	=	she's

we	+	are	=	we're
you	+	are	=	you're
they	+	are	=	they're

E. Change the words. Use the new words from D.

1. **She is** from Vietnam.   She's from Vietnam.

2. **I am** from Vietnam, too.   I'm from Vietnam, too.

3. **We are** in Level 1.   We're in Level 1.

4. **They are** from China.   They're from China.

5. **He is** from Mexico.   He's from Mexico.

8   Unit 1

PREPARATION

If necessary, review the vocabulary
in the language boxes with students
before they open their books.
Preteach the pronoun **we** by moving
your arms to include a student or two
and yourself, and saying, *We are in
English class.* Model the other pro-
nouns by gesturing in similar fashion.

PRESENTATION

A. Have students read the language
boxes independently. Have students
use the words in the language boxes
to say as many sentences as they can.
Explain to students that they can
refer to the language boxes throughout the unit to check or review sentence patterns.

B. Demonstrate by doing the first

item on the board. Have students
complete the activity. Have several
students read the questions and
answers aloud.

C. Have the students complete
the activity. Ask several pairs to
say their conversations to the class.

D. Follow the procedure in A.

E. Follow the procedure in B.

F. Study the examples.

I	my
he	his
she	her
we	our
you	your
they	their

My last name is Bueno.

 G. Work with a small group.
Introduce yourself. Use the words from F.
Say everyone's name.

My name is Elena.
Her name is Sylvia.
His name is Chris.

H. Study the examples.

Where are	you	from?
	they	
Where's	she	
	he	

I'm	from Korea.
She's	
He's	
We're	
They're	

 I. Work with a partner.
Use the sentences in H to talk about the students in
your class.

➤ Where's she from?
● She's from Mexico.

PRESENTATION

F. Follow the procedure in A.

 G. Have students form small groups and complete the activity. Ask several groups to present their introductions to the class.

H. Follow the procedure in A.

 I. Demonstrate how to point out students in class and give information about them to a partner. (You might mention that in the U.S., it is inappropriate to point to someone with the index finger. Discuss alternate ways to indicate someone without pointing a finger, such as gesturing with an open hand.) Then have students complete the activity in pairs. Ask several pairs to present their work to the class.

WORKBOOK

Unit 1, Pages 5–6, Exercises 7A–7D.

FOLLOW-UP

Pronoun Puzzles: Write pairs of sentences like those in E on strips of paper. Cut the strips apart between the sentences. Give students one sentence each and have them circulate around the room until each one finds the student with the "matching" sentence.

♦ Have students use the sentence patterns in G and I to write sentences that name students in the class and tell what countries they are from.

Write It Down

A. Study the names.

Print your name. _____ Pablo Bueno

Sign your name. _____ *Pablo Bueno*
(Signature)

B. Write your name.

Print your name. _____ Answers will vary.

Sign your name. _____
(Signature)

About You **C. Complete the form.**
Write about yourself.

SEATTLE 📖 LIBRARY

APPLICATION FOR CARD

PLEASE PRINT.

Name: _____ Answers will vary.
(LAST)   (FIRST)   (MIDDLE)

Address: _____
(NUMBER AND STREET)   (APT.)

_____
(CITY)

_____
(STATE)   (ZIP CODE)

Telephone: _____
(AREA CODE)   (NUMBER)

Social Security Number: _____

Signature: _____

10   Unit 1

PREPARATION

If necessary, review the vocabulary needed to fill out a form. Follow the instructions in "Preparation" on page 6.

PRESENTATION

Teaching Note: You may want to tell students that they usually won't need Social Security numbers to get library cards. Their passports and letters delivered to them at their homes are usually sufficient identification.

A. Have students compare the printed name and the signature.

B. Have students print and sign their names. Check their work.

About You **C.** Have students look at the form in their books while you complete the form with information about yourself on the board or an overhead transparency. Remind them that they may have blanks on the form if they have no middle names, apartment numbers, or Social Security numbers. Have students fill out the form independently. Have partners compare their completed forms in pairs or small groups. Then check everyone's work.

WORKBOOK

Unit 1, Page 7, Exercise 8.

FOLLOW-UP

Vocabulary Unscramble: Write the key vocabulary words from the application form on several sets of cards. Shuffle each set of cards and give a set to a small group of students to unscramble. The group should use the key words to create a form of its own on a sheet of paper. Have each group show its form to the rest of the class.

♦ Put some examples of identification or application forms on the board or overhead projector and have the class tell you how to fill them out for students in the class.

One To One Student A

I. Practice the dialog.

➤ What's **his** name?
● **Kai Wong.**
➤ How do you spell that?
● **His** first name is **K-A-I. His** last name is **W-O-N-G.**
➤ Where does **he** live?
● **New Jersey.**
➤ Where's **he** from?
● **China.**

 2. Who are they? Ask Student B. Follow the dialog in I. Write the information.

1. Kai Wong
   New Jersey
   China

2. Sylvia Cho
   Florida
   China

3. Pedro Mendoza
   Florida
   Puerto Rico

3. Who are they? Tell Student B. Follow the dialog in I.

4. Steve Jones
   Ohio
   Illinois

5. Maria Garcia
   California
   Texas

6. Binh Do
   New York
   Vietnam

Unit 1   11

Ask for and give personal
information

PREPARATION

If necessary, review spelling aloud by asking where someone lives, and asking about someone's home country. Have students spell their answers aloud.

PRESENTATION

Teaching Note: For more information on these pages, see "One to One" on page vii.

1. Have students find partners. Assign the roles of A and B. Explain that Student A looks only at page A (page 11) and Student B only at page B (page 12). Have them turn to the appropriate pages. Have students talk about the pictures. Then present the dialog. See "Presenting Dialogs" on page vi.

2. Have students read the directions independently. Model the activity with a student. Then have students complete the activity.

3. Have students read the directions independently and complete the activity. Have students switch roles and repeat the activity. (Student A becomes Student B, and B becomes A.) You may want students to switch partners at this time, too. Then check students' answers for both pages.

WORKBOOK

Unit 1, Page 8, Exercise 9.

FOLLOW-UP

Mystery Pictures: Pass out pictures of people cut from magazines or taken from your picture file. Have students work in pairs. Student A holds up a picture and asks questions about the person. Student B makes up appropriate answers for the questions asked. Then students can switch roles. Have pairs of students share their conversations with the class.

♦ Have students write out the questions and answers and share their work with the class.

Ask for and give personal
information

One To One   **Student B**

I. Practice the dialog.

➤ What's **his** name?
● **Kai Wong.**
➤ How do you spell that?
● **His** first name is **K-A-I. His** last name is **W-O-N-G.**
➤ Where does **he** live?
● **New Jersey.**
➤ Where's **he** from?
● **China.**

2. Who are they? Tell Student A. Follow the dialog in I.

1. Kai Wong   2. Sylvia Cho   3. Pedro Mendoza
   New Jersey   Florida   Florida
   China   China   Puerto Rico

 **3. Who are they? Ask Student A. Follow the dialog in I.
Write the information.**

4. <u>Steve Jones</u>   5. <u>Maria Garcia</u>   6. <u>Binh Do</u>
   <u>Ohio</u>   <u>California</u>   <u>New York</u>
   <u>Illinois</u>   <u>Texas</u>   <u>Vietnam</u>

PRESENTATION

Follow the instructions on page 11.

Extension

 A. Practice the dialog.

- ➤ Hello. I'm **Sandy Ryan.**
- ● Nice to meet you, **Sandy.** I'm **Toma Matesa.**
- ➤ Good to meet you, too, **Toma.** Where are you from?
- ● I'm from **Poland.** Are you from **Minnesota?**
- ➤ Yes. Do you live in **Minnesota?**
- ● Yes. I'm a new student.
- ➤ Well, welcome to school.
- ● Thanks.

 B. Work with a partner.
Use the dialog in A to talk about yourself.

 C. Practice the dialog.

- ➤ Hello, **Toma.**
- ● Hi, **Sandy.** How are you?
- ➤ Fine, thanks. How about you?
- ● Fine, thanks.
- ➤ How do you like **Minnesota?**
- ● I really like it.
- ➤ Well, good to see you, **Toma.**
- ● Thanks, **Sandy.** Nice to see you, too.

D. Work with a partner.
Follow the dialog in C.
Talk about yourself.

Unit 1   13

PREPARATION

If possible, have another staff member visit your class. Greet that person as if you are meeting for the first time. Have the person walk out and return. This time greet each other as old friends.

PRESENTATION

A. Have students look at the picture and discuss the different words people use to greet each other. Write their ideas on the board or restate them in acceptable English. Then present the dialog. See "Presenting Dialogs" on page vi.

B. Demonstrate by having a student ask you questions similar to those in A. Have students complete the activity in pairs. Students might change partners and repeat the activity. Ask several pairs to present their conversations to the class.

C. Remind students that old friends greet each other differently from people who are meeting for the first time. Review the differences. Then present the dialog. See "Presenting Dialogs" on page vi.

D. Demonstrate the activity with a student. Have students complete the activity in pairs. Students can switch partners and do the activity again. Have several pairs present their dialogs to the class.

WORKBOOK

Unit 1, Page 8, Exercise 10.

FOLLOW-UP

Greeting Newcomers: Have students work in groups of three or four. Have them imagine themselves as old or new neighbors, and ask them to introduce one another and share personal information. Have groups present their conversations to the class.

◆ Have students write a few sentences they might use to introduce themselves to new neighbors. Have them read their sentences to each other in pairs.

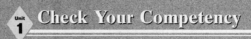

Unit 1 Check Your Competency

Can you use the competencies?

- ☐ 1. Ask for and give personal information
- ☐ 2. Say hello
- ☐ 3. Introduce yourself
- ☐ 4. Complete an identification form

A. Review competencies 1 and 2. Complete the dialog.

✔

| address   area   first   from   name   number   security |

➤ Hello, I need an identification card.

● OK. What's your _____first_____ name and last _____name_____?
➤ **Elena Martinka.**

● What's your ___address___?
➤ **3440 Lake Street, Miami, Florida 33153.**

● Your _____area_____ code and telephone _____number_____?
➤ **(305) 555-1987.**

● Where are you ___from___?
➤ **Russia.**

● What's your Social ___Security___ number?
➤ **281-39-1011.**

Check Up

**Use competencies 1 and 2.
Use the dialog above to talk about yourself.**

14   Unit 1

PRESENTATION

Use any of the procedures in "Evaluation," page viii, with these pages. Record individuals' results on the Unit 1 Individual Competency Chart. Record the class's results on the Class Cumulative Competency Chart.

B. Review competencies 2 and 3. Complete the dialog.

✔

| hello   hi   your   name |

➤ <u>Hello</u>. I'm a new student.

● <u>Hi</u>. My name's **Sylvia.** What's <u>your</u> name?

➤ My <u>name</u> is **Pedro.**

● Good to meet you.

➤ Good to meet you, too.

Check Up
Use competencies 2 and 3.
Use the dialog above to talk about yourself.

Check Up
C. Use competency 4.
Complete the form.

APPLICATION for IDENTIFICATION CARD

Name:_____<u>Answers will vary.</u>_____
        LAST   FIRST

Nationality:_____

Social Security Number:_____

Address:_____
       NUMBER   STREET   APT.

_____
       CITY   STATE   ZIP CODE

Phone:_____
       AREA CODE   PHONE NUMBER

FOLLOW-UP

ENGLISH IN ACTION

An Optional Cooperative Learning Project: You may want to have the class write, produce, and present a short play about a new student at school. The new student will enroll in class, meet new neighbors, and make new friends. (Or, the play might be about a new family in the neighborhood. This would give many opportunities for different types of interactions.)

Have the students collect as much realia as possible to make the play interesting (identification cards, application forms, club membership forms, etc.).

Help students write a script, rehearse, and perform the play. If facilities are available, consider having students audio- or videotape the story. Have them use sound effects (doors opening, papers rustling) to make the production more exciting. Invite the director, an outside guest, or another class to enjoy their production.

Unit 2 Overview

UNIT WARM-UP

The focus of Unit 2, "Our Community," is locations, directions, and reporting emergencies. To stimulate a discussion with students, you might ask them to talk about their experiences getting around when they first came to the U.S. Encourage students to share stories about getting lost.

Unit 2 Optional Materials

● A large map of the area around your school that includes street names and places in the unit, such as stores, banks, etc.

● Picture cards of places and vehicles in a community (ambulance, bank, drug store, fire department, fire truck, gas station, hospital, laundromat, movie theater, park, police station, police car, post office, school, store, supermarket).

● Pictures of a fire and an automobile accident.

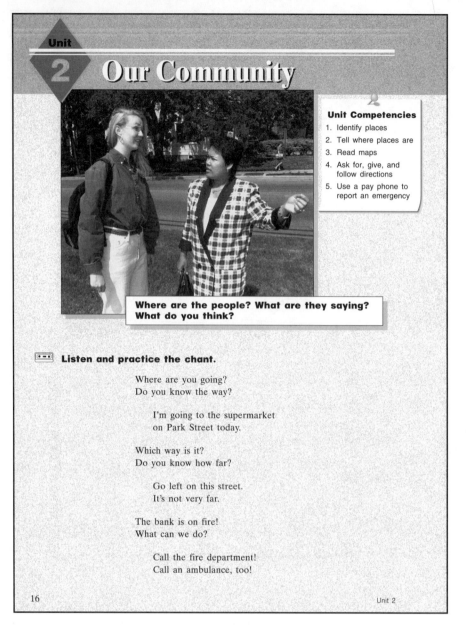

Unit 2

Our Community

Unit Competencies

1. Identify places
2. Tell where places are
3. Read maps
4. Ask for, give, and follow directions
5. Use a pay phone to report an emergency

Where are the people? What are they saying? What do you think?

Listen and practice the chant.

Where are you going?
Do you know the way?

I'm going to the supermarket
on Park Street today.

Which way is it?
Do you know how far?

Go left on this street.
It's not very far.

The bank is on fire!
What can we do?

Call the fire department!
Call an ambulance, too!

16

Unit 2

COMPETENCIES (page 16)

Identify places

Tell where places are

Ask for, give, and follow directions

PREPARATION

Use pantomime, picture cards, and the map to preteach the new language. Follow these suggestions.

● Hold up each picture card and name the place or vehicle to present **bank, supermarket, fire department,** and **ambulance.** Have students repeat.

● For asking and giving directions, use the map. Give directions to a place near your school. Say, *Go (right) on this street* as you describe the route and trace it on the map.

● For reporting emergencies, show a picture of a fire. Say, *There's a fire! Call the fire department.* Pantomime making a telephone call.

● You may also want to preteach: **Where are you going? Do you know the way? I'm going to the (bank).**

PREPARATION

Focus attention on the photo and have students answer the questions. Encourage them to say everything they can about it. Write their ideas on the board or restate them in acceptable English.

Present the chant. See "Presenting Chants" on page vi.

WORKBOOK

Unit 2, Page 9, Exercise 1.

FOLLOW-UP

Dialogs: Have pairs of students use the map you made to make up dialogs in which they ask and answer questions about the places. Have several pairs of students present their dialogs to the class.

♦ Have students write their dialogs.

Real-Life English

Starting Out

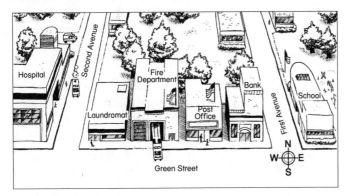

 A. Practice the dialog.

➤ Where's the **bank?**
● It's next to the **post office.**
➤ Is it **between** the **laundromat** and the **post office?**
● No, it isn't. It's **on the corner of First Avenue and Green Street.**
➤ Is the **bank across from the school?**
● Yes, it is.

B. Complete the sentences. Use the map in A.

1. The laundromat is next to the ____fire department____.

2. The fire department is between the laundromat and the

____post office____.

3. The ____hospital____ is across from the laundromat.

4. The ____school____ is on First Avenue.

C. Work with a partner.
Where do you want to go?
Use the dialog in A to talk about places on the map.

PREPARATION

Use picture cards and the map you used with page 16 to preteach the new language. Follow these suggestions.

● To present the places on the Student Book page, hold up each picture card and name the place. Have students say the names after you. Use the map to present **on the corner.**

● Model **next to, between,** and **across from.** Have two students join you in front of the class. Stand at the end of the row. Say, *I am next to (name).* Repeat with **between** and **across from.** Then have students form two facing rows of three students each at the front of the class. Ask, *Where's (name)?* Have students

continue asking and answering questions.

PRESENTATION

A. Have students talk about the map. Encourage them to say everything they can about it. Write their ideas on the board or restate them in acceptable English. Ask students what the compass means. Then present the dialog. See "Presenting Dialogs" on page vi.

B. Demonstrate by doing the first item on the board. Have students complete the activity independently. Ask several students to read their answers aloud.

Teaching Note: Help students generalize that, in the dialog, the names of places are written in lowercase let-

ters. Remind them to write the places in lowercase letters in their answers.

C. Demonstrate by having a student ask you questions similar to those in A. Have students complete the activity. Then have students switch partners and repeat the activity. Have several pairs of students present their conversations to the class.

WORKBOOK

Unit 2, Page 9, Exercise 2.

FOLLOW-UP

Questions and Answers: Have pairs of students ask and answer questions about places on the map. Have several pairs select some of their questions to ask the class.

◆ Have students write questions and ask others to answer them in writing.

Identify places

Tell where places are

Read maps

Ask for, give, and follow directions

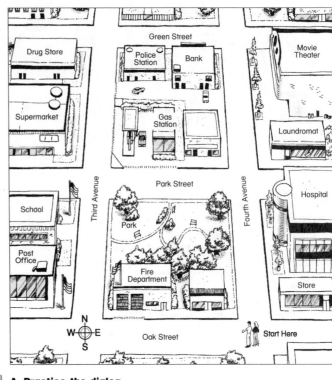

Talk It Over

 A. Practice the dialog.

> ➤ Excuse me. Where's the **police station?**
> ● It's **one block** north of the **park.**
> ➤ Where?
> ● **One block north** of the **park,** on **Green Street.**
> ➤ **One block north** of the **park,** on **Green Street.** Thanks.

**B. Work with a partner.
Where do you want to go?
Use the dialog in A to ask for directions
to places on the map.**

18   Unit 2

PREPARATION

Make and display signs of the directions **north, south, east,** and **west** and use the picture cards and map you used with page 16 to preteach the new language. Follow these suggestions.

● Label the walls of your room with their directions: north, south, east, and west. Place one picture card at each wall. Walk around the classroom and hold up each card in turn as you describe its location. Say, *The (park) is (north) of the (school).* Have students repeat. Then present the abbreviations **N, S, E,** and **W.** Have students match the abbreviations and the directions.

● Use the picture cards to preteach or review the places on the map in the Student Book. Use the map you made to explain **block.**

PRESENTATION

A. Have students talk about the map. Encourage them to say everything they can about it. If necessary, draw attention to the compass and ask students to talk about it. Write their ideas on the board or restate them in acceptable English. Then present the dialog. See "Presenting Dialogs" on page vi.

B. Demonstrate by having a student ask you questions similar to those in A. Have students complete the activity. Then have students switch partners and repeat the activity. Ask several pairs of students to present their conversations to the class.

WORKBOOK

Unit 2, Page 10, Exercise 3.

FOLLOW-UP

North, South, East, and West: Have students in small groups ask each other questions such as *Is the supermarket south of the school?* Have them check their answers on the map.

♦ Have each student write one or two questions about the locations of places, ask another student, and record the answers.

Word Bank

A. Study the vocabulary.

Places	store		
bank	supermarket		
drug store			
fire department	accident		
gas station	fire		
hospital			
laundromat	ambulance		
movie theater	fire truck		
park	police car	north	block
police station		south	corner
post office	left	east	
school	right	west	

Useful Language
Go (north).
Turn (right).
How do I get (there)?
There's a (fire).

B. Complete the dialog.
Use the map on page 18. Use words from A.

➤ How do I get to the **bank** from here?

● Go **two blocks** _____ north _____ on **Fourth** _____ Avenue _____.

Turn _____ left _____ on **Green Street.**

The **bank** is **on the** _____ corner _____ of **Fourth Avenue** and **Green Street.**

 C. Work with a partner.
Where do you want to go?
Use the dialog in B to ask for directions to places
on the map on page 18.

COMPETENCIES (page 19)
Identify places
Tell where places are
Read maps
Ask for, give, and follow directions

PREPARATION
Preteach or review the new vocabulary before students open their books. Give special attention to **accident, fire truck, police car, go,** and **turn,** which are first presented on this page. Use the picture cards and map you used with page 16. Provide any reinforcement necessary. See "Reinforcing Vocabulary" on page vi.

PRESENTATION
A. Have students scan the list. Define, or have students define, any words individuals do not recognize. Provide any reinforcement necessary. See "Reinforcing Vocabulary" on page vi. Remind students that they can use this list throughout the unit to look up words, to check spelling, and to find key phrases.

B. Have students look back at the map on page 18. Encourage them to say everything they can about it. Have students find the starting place. Make sure students understand that they should use words from A to complete the exercise. Have students complete the activity independently. Have several students read their answers aloud while other students check their own answers.

C. Demonstrate by having a student ask you questions similar to those in B. Have students complete the activity. Then have students switch partners and repeat the activity. Ask several pairs of students to present their conversations to the class.

WORKBOOK
Unit 2, Page 11, Exercises 4A–4B.

FOLLOW-UP
Everyday Places: Have small groups of students talk about the places they go during the week or on the weekend. Encourage students to describe each place and its location. Have the groups summarize their discussions for the class.

♦ Students can write a list of the places they go to and read the list aloud as they share their ideas with the class.

Identify places

Tell where places are

Read maps

Ask for, give, and follow directions

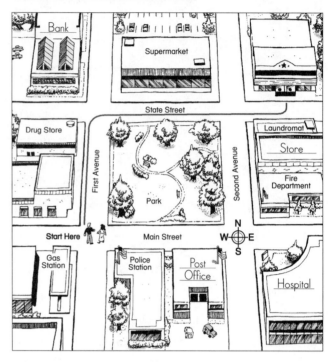

Listening

 A. Look, listen, and write the places on the map.

| bank   hospital   post office   store |

B. Look, listen, and follow the directions.
Draw a line on the map.

 C. Where do you want to go?
Ask a partner for directions.
Draw a line on the map.

20   Unit 2

PREPARATION

If necessary, review the place names, the prepositions of location, and language used for giving directions. Use the picture cards and map you used with page 16. Have students name places, say where they are in relation to one another on the map, and give each other directions to the places. Provide any reinforcement necessary. See "Reinforcing Vocabulary" on page vi.

PRESENTATION

Teaching Note: You may want to have colored pencils available for students to use to show the different routes they will draw for Exercises B and C.

A. Have students read the directions. Make sure students understand that they will write the words from the box on the map. Have students complete the activity as you play the tape or read the

Listening Transcript aloud two or more times. Check students' work.

B. Have students complete the activity independently as you play the tape or read the Listening Transcript aloud two or more times. Check students' work.

C. Demonstrate by asking, *I want to go to the (store). How do I get there?* to a student. Have the student give you directions as you draw the route on the map in your book. Have students complete the activity in pairs. Have several pairs of students share their maps with the class.

WORKBOOK

Unit 2, Page 12, Exercise 5.

FOLLOW-UP

Where Are You Going? Have students mark a new starting point on the map to play this game. Demonstrate by giving directions to a place on the map, without identifying the destination in advance. Have the class listen, follow the directions, and then identify where they end up. Then have volunteers give directions to other places on the map, and have the class identify the destinations.

♦ Have students work in pairs to write simple directions to places near school. Have them exchange directions with other pairs of students. Can students follow each other's directions?

Reading

A. Look and read.

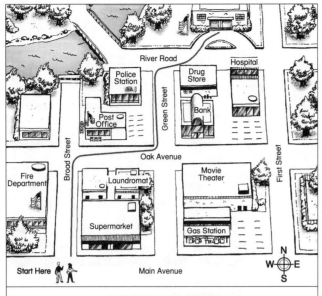

ADULT LEARNING CENTER
English Program–New Student Registration
Wednesday, August 15th 9:00 A.M.–5:00 P.M.
225 River Road

Directions: From Broad Street and Main Avenue, go north on Broad Street. Turn right on Oak Avenue. Go one block. Turn left on Green Street. Go one block north. Turn right on River Road. The school is on the left, across from the hospital.

B. Answer the questions.

1. What can you study at the Adult Learning Center? <u>English</u>

2. What's the address of the Adult Learning Center? <u>225 River Road</u>

 C. Follow the directions to the school in A.
Draw a line on the map.

COMPETENCIES (page 21)

Identify places
Tell where places are
Read maps
Ask for, give, and follow directions

PREPARATION

If necessary, review the place names, prepositions of location, and language used for giving directions. Follow the instructions in "Preparation" on page 20.

Culture Note: Explain that in the U.S., community groups often hold meetings in public buildings because those buildings usually have large meeting rooms. Have students name some community groups they are familiar with. Where do they meet?

PRESENTATION

A. Have students preview the notice for a few minutes before they read it. See "Prereading" on page vii. Encourage them to say everything they can about the notice. Write

their ideas on the board or restate them in acceptable English. Ask students what the compass means. Then have them read the notice independently.

B. Have students read and answer the questions orally and then in writing. Remind them that an **address** usually includes a number and a street name. Have several students say their answers aloud.

C. Have students read and complete the activity independently. Check students' work.

WORKBOOK

Unit 2, Page 12, Exercise 6.

FOLLOW-UP

New Notices: Have students work in

small groups to create new notices similar to the one on page 21 for a class party, an open house, or a class trip. Encourage them to select real places in the community and to write directions from the school to the places.

♦ Have students bring in real maps and directions from newspapers or telephone directories. Have them use the directions to create sale fliers, notices, or ads of their own.

Identify places

Tell where places are

Read maps

Ask for, give, and follow directions

Structure Base

A. Study the examples.

Am	I	on Main Street?
Is	he	
	she	
	it	
Are	we	
	you	
	they	

Yes,	I am.
	he	is.
	she	
	it	
	we	are.
	you	
	they	

No,	I'm not.
	he	isn't.
	she	
	it	
	we	aren't.
	you	
	they	

OAK AVENUE

OPEN

B. Look at the picture. Answer the questions. Use words from A.

1. Is she at the post office?   _No, she isn't._

2. Is she at the drug store?   _No, she isn't_

3. Is she at the store?   _Yes, she is._

4. Is the store on Park Street?   _No, it isn't._

5. Is the store on Oak Avenue?   _Yes, it is._

22   Unit 2

PREPARATION

If necessary, review the vocabulary in the language boxes with students before they open their books. Follow the instructions in "Preparation" on page 20.

PRESENTATION

A. Have students read the language boxes independently. Have students use the words in the language boxes to say as many sentences as they can. Explain to students that they can refer to the language boxes throughout the unit to check or review sentence patterns.

B. Demonstrate by doing the first item on the board. Have students complete the activity. Have several students read the questions and answers aloud.

C. Study the examples.

The fire department is	on Main Street.
	on the corner of Main and Oak.
	next to the police station.
	between the police station and the school.
	across from the movie theater.

 D. Work with a small group.
   Use the sentences in C to talk about places in your city or town.

E. Study the example.

Where's the fire department?

 F. Work with a partner.
   Talk about places in your city or town.

> ➤ Where's the **drug store?**
> ● It's **on First Avenue.**
> ➤ Is it **next to the movie theater?**
> ● **Yes, it is.**

G. Study the examples.

an	accident		a	hospital
	emergency			police car

H. Complete the sentences. Write *a* or *an.*

> ➤ Oh, no! <u>An</u> accident! Call <u>an</u> ambulance.

> ● Yes, call <u>a</u> fire truck, too.

> ★ OK. Where's <u>a</u> phone?

PRESENTATION

C. Follow the procedure in A.

 D. Demonstrate by describing the location of a place you know. Then have students complete the activity. Then have students form new groups and repeat the activity. Ask several pairs of students to present their conversations to the class.

E. Follow the procedure in A.

 F. Have students complete the activity. Ask several pairs of students to present their conversations to the class.

G. Follow the procedure in A.

H. Demonstrate by doing the first item on the board. Then have students complete the activity independently. Have two students read the sentences aloud as the rest of the class checks the answers.

WORKBOOK

Unit 2, Pages 13–15, Exercises 7A–7D.

FOLLOW-UP

Where Am I? Have students use the map on page 21 to play this game. Demonstrate by choosing a location and giving three sentences as clues. Say, *I'm on (street). I'm across from the (place). I'm next to the (place). Where am I?* (the movie theater). Divide the class into small groups and have them play the game until each student has had a chance to give clues.

♦ Have students write three clues on cards for each location on the map. Then have them play the game in small groups by drawing cards one at a time, reading the clues aloud, and identifying the places.

Identify places

Tell where places are

Read maps

Ask for, give, and follow directions

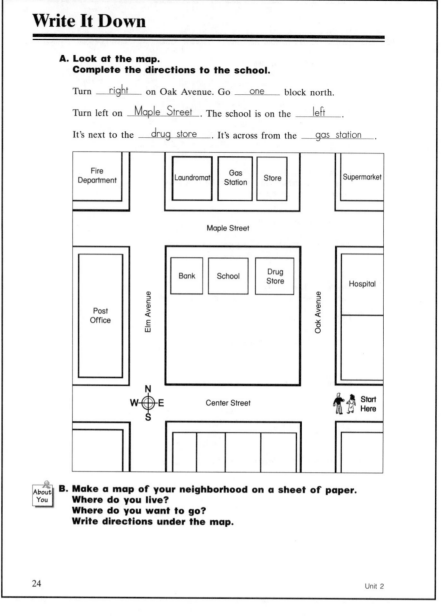

Write It Down

**A. Look at the map.
Complete the directions to the school.**

Turn ___right___ on Oak Avenue. Go ___one___ block north.

Turn left on ___Maple Street___. The school is on the ___left___.

It's next to the ___drug store___. It's across from the ___gas station___.

**B. Make a map of your neighborhood on a sheet of paper.
Where do you live?
Where do you want to go?
Write directions under the map.**

24   Unit 2

PREPARATION

If necessary, review the place names, prepositions of location, and language used for giving directions. Follow the instructions in "Preparation" on page 20.

PRESENTATION

Teaching Note: You may want to explain to students the importance of proofreading directions to be sure that people following the directions don't get lost.

A. Have students talk about the map. Encourage them to say everything they can about it. Write their ideas on the board or restate them in acceptable English. Ask them to find the starting point. Ask students what the compass indicates. Have students complete the activity independently. Ask several students to read the completed directions while the rest of the students trace the route on their maps with their fingers.

B. Use the map you used with page 16. Say, *I want to go to the (place).* Demonstrate how to get to the place. Then write the directions on the board. Have students complete the activity independently. Have pairs of students compare and talk about their maps and directions. Ask several students to share their maps and directions with the class.

WORKBOOK

Unit 2, Page 15, Exercise 8.

FOLLOW-UP

Local Maps: Prepare enough simple maps of your community for each pair of students. Mark a different place on each map. Distribute the maps and have pairs of students write directions to the places. Have students display their maps and directions.

♦ Have students work in pairs to create community maps using places they know about. Then have them write directions to places on their maps. Have them share their maps and directions with other pairs of students and/or the rest of the class.

One To One   Student A

I. Practice the dialog.

> ➤ Excuse me. Where's the **fire department**?
> ● It's **north of the post office**.
> ➤ Where?
> ● **North of the post office**.
>   It's **on First Avenue, across from the bank**.
> ➤ **On First Avenue, across from the bank.** Thanks.

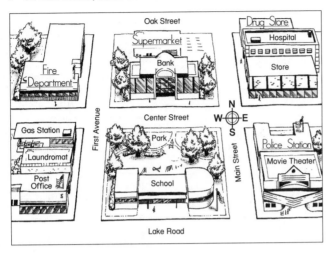

 2. Ask Student B for directions. Follow the dialog in I.
Write the places on the map.

the fire department
the police station
the supermarket
the drug store

 3. Give Student B directions.
Use the map. Follow the dialog in I.

4. Switch roles. Turn to page 26. Complete 2 and 3.

Unit 2   25

Tell where places are

Read maps

Ask for, give, and follow directions

PREPARATION

If necessary, review the place names, prepositions of location, and language used for giving directions. Follow the instructions in "Preparation" on page 20.

PRESENTATION

Teaching Note: For more information on these pages, see "One to One" on page vii.

1. Have students find partners. Assign the roles of A and B. Explain that Student A looks only at page A (page 25) and Student B only at page B (page 26). Have them turn to the appropriate pages. Have students talk about the map. Encourage them to name the streets. Have everyone locate the fire department. Then present the dialog. See "Presenting Dialogs" on page vi.

2. Have students read the directions independently. Model the activity with a student. Then have students complete the activity.

3. Have students read the directions independently and complete the activity.

4. Have students read the directions and complete the activity. (You may want students to switch partners at this time, too.) Then check students' answers for both pages.

WORKBOOK

Unit 2, Page 16, Exercise 9.

FOLLOW-UP

Where Is It? Have students work in pairs (Student A, Student B) to draw a simple map of an imaginary community, labeling the streets but leaving the buildings unlabeled. Then have Student A ask, *Where is the (place)?* Student B should then choose a location on the map and give directions to it so that Student A can label it. Partners can switch roles and continue, labeling as many buildings as they can. Have several pairs of students display their maps and describe their imaginary communities to the class.

♦ Have students write the directions they hear, and then use the written directions to locate places on the map.

Tell where places are

Read maps

Ask for, give, and follow directions

One To One   **Student B**

I. Practice the dialog.

➤ Excuse me. Where's the **fire department?**
● It's **north of the post office.**
➤ Where?
● **North of the post office.**
  It's **on First Avenue, across from the bank.**
➤ **On First Avenue, across from the bank.** Thanks.

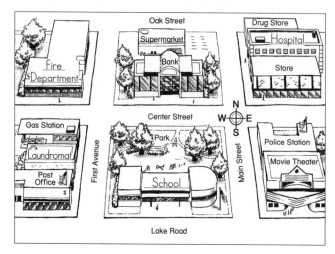

 2. Give Student A directions.
Use the map. Follow the dialog in I.

 3. Ask Student A for directions. Follow the dialog in I.
Write the places on the map.

the hospital
the laundromat
the school

4. Switch roles. Turn to page 25. Complete 2 and 3.

26   Unit 2

PRESENTATION

Follow the instructions on page 25.

Extension

 A. Practice the dialog.

➤ Oh, no! An accident!
   Find a telephone.
● OK.

➤ Pick up the telephone.
   Dial 911.
   Say that there's an accident.

★ Parkview, Lake County 911.
● There's an accident.
   Please send an ambulance.

★ Where's the accident?
● 410 Green Street.
★ OK. We'll be right there.

B. Work with a partner.
Use the dialog in A to report other emergencies.

Unit 2   27

PRESENTATION

● Hold up pictures of an **accident** and a **fire** and name each one. Have students repeat. Name, or have students name, the emergency services that respond to each kind of emergency.

● Display a picture of a pay phone and identify it.

Culture Note: Explain to students that a 911 call from a pay phone does not require a coin deposit. You may want to explain how to use a pay phone, teaching words such as **deposit, coin slot, receiver, dial tone, dial,** and **coin return.**

PRESENTATION

A. Have students talk about the pictures. Encourage them to say every-thing they can about them. Write their ideas on the board or restate them in acceptable English. Then present the dialog. See "Presenting Dialogs" on page vi.

B. Brainstorm with the class possible emergency situations, such as a grass fire at a park, a sick person at the laundromat, or a minor car accident. Make the situations realistic, but non-threatening. Demonstrate the activity with a student. Have students complete the activity in pairs. Have students switch partners and repeat the activity. Have pairs of students present their conversations to the class.

WORKBOOK

Unit 2, Page 16, Exercise 10.

FOLLOW-UP

Other Emergencies: Help the class brainstorm other possible emergencies, such as robberies, purse snatchings, etc. Supply any vocabulary students need. You may want to discuss with the class precautions they can take to avoid these situations.

◆ Have students role-play 911 calls for the emergencies they just brainstormed. Encourage students to include language from Unit 1 in their conversation, such as giving their names and addresses. Invite students to present their conversations to the class.

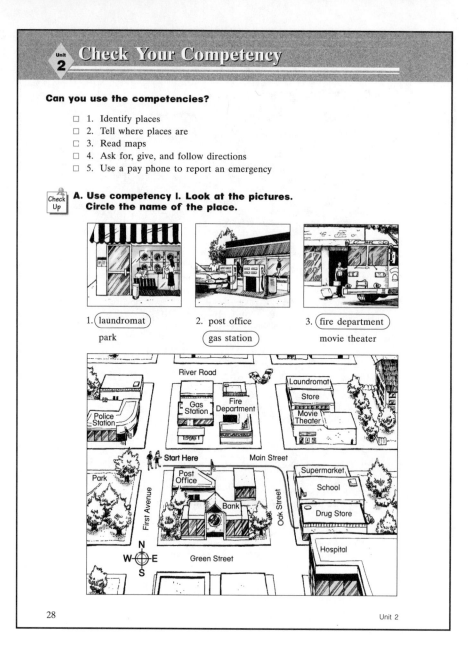

Can you use the competencies?

- ☐ 1. Identify places
- ☐ 2. Tell where places are
- ☐ 3. Read maps
- ☐ 4. Ask for, give, and follow directions
- ☐ 5. Use a pay phone to report an emergency

Check Up

A. Use competency I. Look at the pictures. Circle the name of the place.

1. (laundromat)
   park

2. post office
   (gas station)

3. (fire department)
   movie theater

28   Unit 2

PROCEDURES

Use any of the procedures in "Evaluation," page viii, with these pages. For exercise C, play the tape or read the Listening Transcript aloud two or more times. Record individuals' results on the Unit 1 Individual Competency Chart. Record the class's results on the Class Cumulative Competency Chart.

B. Review competencies 2, 3, and 4. Complete the dialog.
Use the map on page 28.
✔

| block   east   left   next to |

➤ Excuse me. Where's the **store?**

● Go **one block** _____east_____ on **Main Street.** Turn

_____left_____ . Go **one** _____block_____ **north** on **Oak Street.**

The **store** is _____next to_____ the **movie theater.**

➤ OK. Thanks.

Check Up
Use competencies 2, 3, and 4.
Use the dialog in B to give directions
to another place on the map on page 28.

Check Up
C. Use competency 4.
Listen to the directions.
Draw a line on the map on page 28.

D. Review competency 5. Complete the dialog.
✔

| accident   ambulance   telephone   911 |

➤ There's **an accident!** Find a _____telephone_____ . Dial _____911_____ .

● **Fairview, Lake County 911.**

➤ There's **an** _____accident_____ at **River Road and Oak Street.**

Send **an** _____ambulance_____ .

Check Up
Use competency 5.
Use the dialog above to report another emergency.

FOLLOW-UP

ENGLISH IN ACTION

An Optional Cooperative Learning Project: You may want to have students work together to create a directory of community facilities for new students. First, help students create a list of the places that they want to include. Then help them decide what to include about each place, such as maps, drawings of each place, written directions to each place, and emergency calling procedures. Have small groups of students choose to be responsible for one or more of the places. Help students decide on an organizational scheme and put their pages together in a notebook. Have one or two new students use the directory and report to the class on how it helped them.

Unit 3 Overview

UNIT WARM-UP

The focus of Unit 3, "School and Country," is schools and education. To stimulate a discussion with students, use your classroom environment. Talk about the desks, books, and other classroom objects, the room, and the school staff. You might ask students about their own and/or their children's school experiences. Encourage them to discuss the importance of knowing about school activities and facilities, as parents of children in school or as students themselves.

Unit 3 Optional Materials

● Pictures cut out of magazines labeled to represent school personnel (counselor, secretary, director, teacher), adult students, and school-children.

● Notebooks, pens, pencils, and so on to familiarize students with school supplies.

● A large map similar to those on pages 32 and 34 to focus the discussion on building directories and the locations of places in buildings.

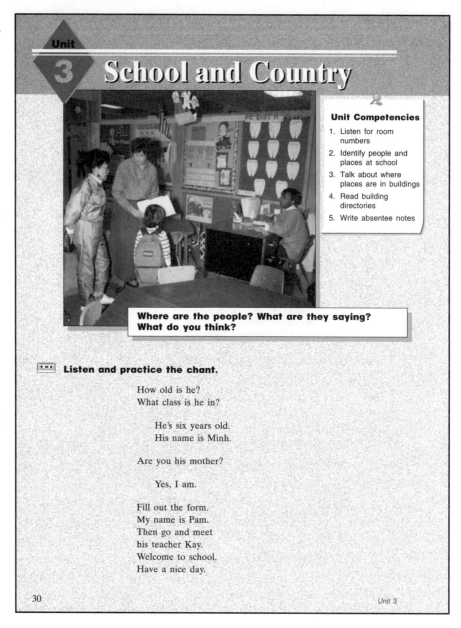

Unit 3

School and Country

Unit Competencies

1. Listen for room numbers
2. Identify people and places at school
3. Talk about where places are in buildings
4. Read building directories
5. Write absentee notes

Where are the people? What are they saying? What do you think?

Listen and practice the chant.

How old is he?
What class is he in?

He's six years old.
His name is Minh.

Are you his mother?

Yes, I am.

Fill out the form.
My name is Pam.
Then go and meet
his teacher Kay.
Welcome to school.
Have a nice day.

30

Unit 3

COMPETENCIES (page 30)

Identify people and places at school

PREPARATION

Use pictures to preteach the new language in the chant. Follow these suggestions.

● Hold up the pictures of the teacher and the secretary (or use pictures in the book) and say their titles. Have students repeat their titles after you. Hold up the pictures of schoolchildren. Invite students to name any schoolchildren they know.

● Preteach the questions in the chant: **How old is he? What class is he in? Are you his mother?**

Culture Note: You might want to tell students that in the U.S., elementary

teachers ask children to address them by title (Ms., Miss, Mrs., Mr.) and last name. Some teachers of adults in the U.S. prefer that students call them by their first names. Students who are uncomfortable doing so may use the formal address of title and last name.

You may want to explain that children ages 6–12 attend elementary school.

PRESENTATION

Focus attention on the photo and have students answer the questions. Encourage them to say everything they can about it. Write their ideas on the board or restate them in acceptable English.

Present the chant. See "Presenting Chants" on page vi.

WORKBOOK

Unit 3, Page 17, Exercise 1.

FOLLOW-UP

Family Photos: Invite students to bring in pictures of their children or their relatives' children. Have students work in pairs to talk about the names and ages of the children, their classes or grades in school, and their teachers. Have several pairs present their conversations to the class.

◆ Have each student write about one child and read the information to the class.

Starting Out

A. Look, listen, and read.

In the U.S. all children have to go to school starting at age 6.
Today is Anh Luc's first day in school.

1. Anh's talking to his teacher.

2. Alma and Chen are opening the windows.

3. Sarita's sharpening pencils.

4. Binh, Alma, and Miguel are reading. Jesse's writing.

 B. Answer the questions.

1. What are the children doing?
2. Is this school like the schools in your country? Explain.

Unit 3   31

PREPARATION

Use the pictures of schoolchildren and the school supplies to preteach the new language. Follow these suggestions.

● Hold up the pictures of schoolchildren and talk about the different activities children might participate in at school. Have students offer additional activities.

● Pantomime the verbs in the vocabulary. Pantomime writing in a notebook as you say, *I'm writing in a notebook.* Model the question *What are you doing?* Then have students ask you. Answer, *I'm writing in a notebook.* Repeat the procedure with the remaining new language. Then have volunteers follow the same procedure.

Culture Note: You may want to explain to students that adult schools often teach ESL, ABE (Adult Basic Education), GED (General Educational Development), career education, etc. Explain that an elementary school has a principal; an adult school usually has a director.

PRESENTATION

A. Have students talk about the pictures. Encourage students to say everything they can about them. Write their ideas on the board or restate them in acceptable English. Then play the tape or read the captions aloud as students follow along in their books. Have students read the captions again independently.

B. Have the class discuss the questions in B. Help students compare and contrast their own school experiences.

WORKBOOK

Unit 3, Page 18, Exercise 2.

FOLLOW-UP

Mime Game: Have students work in small groups. Have students take turns performing actions while the others identify each action. Have students say *You're reading.* Continue until everyone has performed or identified an action.

♦ As students pantomime actions, have other students write sentences identifying the actions. Have students read their sentences aloud.

Listen for room numbers

Identify people and places at school

Talk about where places are in buildings

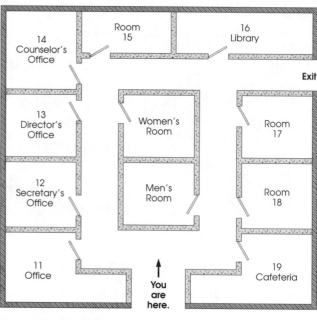

Talk It Over

 A. Today is Miguel Soto's first day at City Learning Center. Practice the dialog.

➤ Excuse me. Where's the **director's office?**
● Room **13.**
➤ Room **13?**
● Yes, **13.**
➤ How do I get there?
● Go **left.** Go **around the corner** and **down the hall.** It's on the **left.**
➤ Thanks.
● You're welcome.

**B. Work with a partner.
Where do you want to go?
Use the dialog in A to talk about places on the map.**

32   Unit 3

PREPARATION

Use the pictures of school personnel and the large map you made to preteach the new language. Follow these suggestions.

● Display the map and the labeled pictures of school personnel. Briefly explain what their jobs are and point out their offices on the map. Point out the classrooms on the map as you identify the teachers and the students.

● Use the map to give directions to a room in the building. Trace the route with your hand as you give the directions. Invite volunteers to ask you where other rooms are on the map. Respond by giving directions.

PRESENTATION

A. Have students talk about the map. Encourage them to say everything they can about it. Write their ideas on the board or restate them in acceptable English. Then present the dialog. See "Presenting Dialogs" on page vi.

B. Demonstrate by having a student ask you questions similar to those in A. Have students complete the activity. Then have them switch partners and repeat the activity. Ask several pairs to present their dialogs to the class.

WORKBOOK

Unit 3, Page 18, Exercise 3.

FOLLOW-UP

Giving Directions: Draw a simple school map similar to the one on this page and make copies. Give one map to each pair of students. Ask one partner to give directions to a room without identifying it and ask the other partner to follow the directions and name the room. Have volunteers give directions to the whole class and see if everyone names the same room.

♦ Follow the steps in "Giving Directions," but have pairs of students write directions instead of saying them. Have each partner read the other's directions and try to arrive at the correct room.

Listen for room numbers

Talk about where places are in buildings

Word Bank

A. Study the vocabulary.

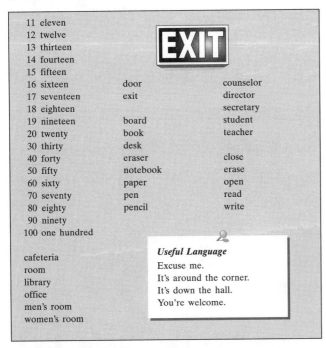

11 eleven		
12 twelve		
13 thirteen		
14 fourteen		
15 fifteen		
16 sixteen	door	counselor
17 seventeen	exit	director
18 eighteen		secretary
19 nineteen	board	student
20 twenty	book	teacher
30 thirty	desk	
40 forty	eraser	close
50 fifty	notebook	erase
60 sixty	paper	open
70 seventy	pen	read
80 eighty	pencil	write
90 ninety		
100 one hundred		

cafeteria
room
library
office
men's room
women's room

Useful Language
Excuse me.
It's around the corner.
It's down the hall.
You're welcome.

B. Look at the map on page 32. Complete the dialog. Use words from the list in A.

➤ Where's the **director's** office?

● Room ____13____. Turn ____left____. Go

____around____ **the corner.**

➤ Thanks.

 C. Work with a partner.
Use the dialog in B to talk about places in your school.

Unit 3   33

PREPARATION

Preteach or review the new vocabulary before students open their books. Give special attention to the number words and the words **door, exit, board, desk, eraser, paper, pen, close,** and **erase.** Use school items, pictures, and the map you used with page 32. To introduce and review verbs, use the technique you used with page 31. Provide any reinforcement necessary. See "Reinforcing Vocabulary" on page vi.

PRESENTATION

A. Have students scan the list. Define, or have other students define, any words individuals do not recognize. Provide any reinforcement necessary. See "Reinforcing

Vocabulary" on page vi. Remind students that they can use this list throughout the unit to look up words, to check spelling, and to find key phrases.

B. Have students look back at the map on page 32. Encourage them to say everything they can about it. Have students find the starting place. Make sure students understand that they should use the words from the box to complete the exercise. Have students complete the activity independently. Have several students read their answers aloud while the class checks the directions on the map.

C. Demonstrate by having a student ask you questions similar to those in B. Have students com-

plete the activity. Then have students switch partners and repeat the activity. Ask several pairs of students to present their dialogs to the class.

WORKBOOK

Unit 3, Page 19, Exercises 4A–4C.

FOLLOW-UP

Everyday Routes: Have students work in pairs to draw simple maps of the building where the class is held. Remind them to put room numbers on their maps and mark starting points. Have partners take turns telling each other how to get to different rooms in the building. Have pairs of students share their maps with the class.

◆ Have each pair of students write directions to one room on their map. Have them show their map and read their directions to the class.

Identify people and places at school

Talk about where places are in buildings

Listening

A. Look, listen, and write the room numbers.

1. Level 1 English — II
2. Level 2 English — I5
3. Level 3 English — 20
4. Level 4 English — 27

B. Look, listen, and write the room numbers on the map.

CAFETERIA 17

DIRECTOR 16

EXIT

SECRETARY 14

COUNSELORS 19

COMPUTER ROOM 20

OFFICE 10

WOMEN

You are here.

MEN

C. Look, listen, and follow the directions. Draw a line on the map.

34

Unit 3

PREPARATION

If necessary, review place names, names of school personnel, and the language used for asking and giving directions. Use the map you used on page 32. Have students name places, say room numbers, and give each other directions to places on the map. Provide any reinforcement necessary. See "Reinforcing Vocabulary" on page vi.

Teaching Note: You may want to explain to students that syllable stress helps distinguish between number words: numbers ending in **-teen (thirteen)** are stressed on the second syllable, numbers ending in **-ty (thirty)** are stressed on the first.

PRESENTATION

A, B, and **C.** Have students listen and complete the activities independently as you play the tape or read the Listening Transcript aloud two or more times. Check students' work.

WORKBOOK

Unit 3, Page 20, Exercise 5.

FOLLOW-UP

Finding the Way: Divide the class into small groups. Have students tell about how they found their way to class the first time. Have each group choose one story to tell the rest of the class.

♦ Have students write a few sentences about how they found their way to class the first time. Have volunteers read their sentences to the class.

Reading

A. Look and read.

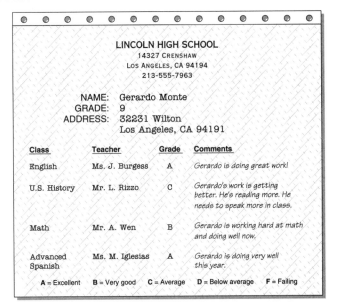

LINCOLN HIGH SCHOOL
14327 CRENSHAW
LOS ANGELES, CA 94194
213-555-7963

NAME: Gerardo Monte
GRADE: 9
ADDRESS: 32231 Wilton
Los Angeles, CA 94191

Class	Teacher	Grade	Comments
English	Ms. J. Burgess	A	Gerardo is doing great work!
U.S. History	Mr. L. Rizzo	C	Gerardo's work is getting better. He's reading more. He needs to speak more in class.
Math	Mr. A. Wen	B	Gerardo is working hard at math and doing well now.
Advanced Spanish	Ms. M. Iglesias	A	Gerardo is doing very well this year.

A = Excellent   **B** = Very good   **C** = Average   **D** = Below average   **F** = Failing

B. Answer the questions about Gerardo Monte's grade report.

1. How many A's did he get?   2
2. How many B's did he get?   1
3. How many C's did he get?   1

C. Work with a partner. Answer the questions.

1. Which classes is Gerardo doing well in?
2. Does he need to study more in math?
3. Gerardo's mother wants to talk to his English teacher. What's her name?
4. Do you think Gerardo's a good student?
5. Do you have children? How are their grades?

Unit 3   35

PREPARATION

Preteach or review the new vocabulary. If necessary, define **grade** and **grade report.** Explain that grades are given for individual classes. Provide any reinforcement necessary. See "Reinforcing Vocabulary" on page vi.

Culture Note: You may want to explain that in the U.S., students often receive grade reports four times or more in a school year. Explain the A, B, C, D, F system and what passing and failing grades are.

You might tell students that summer school is an option for students who need extra help. Some schools offer free tutoring, especially for ESL students.

PRESENTATION

A. Have students preview the grade report for a few minutes before they read it. See "Prereading" on page vii. Encourage them to say everything they can about the report. Write their ideas on the board or restate them in acceptable English. Then have them read the grade report independently.

B. Have students read and complete the activity independently. Check students' work.

C. Have students complete the activity in pairs. Then ask students to say their answers aloud.

WORKBOOK

Unit 3, Page 20, Exercise 6.

FOLLOW-UP

Grade Reports: Create three or four grade reports similar to the one in this lesson. (Or, ask students to bring their children's grade reports to share with the class.) Divide the class into small groups and give each group a report. Have students in each group read their report and tell the rest of the class about it.

♦ Post three or four grade reports around the room. Have students look at them and write questions to ask the rest of the class about them, such as *Who's taking French? Who has three A's? Who needs to work harder?*

Structure Base

A. Study the examples.

I'm	reading a book.
He's	
She's	
We're	
You're	
They're	

I'm not		reading a book.
He	isn't	
She		
We	aren't	
You		
They		

B. Write the correct form of the word.

1. Mei's meeting _____ (**meet**) the teacher.

2. The students aren't talking _____ (**not talking**).

   They're studying _____ (**study**).

3. Arnulfo and Lee are sharpening _____ (**sharpen**) their pencils.

4. David's closing _____ (**close**) the window.

5. Mei isn't reading _____ (**not read**) a book.

   She's reading _____ (**read**) a magazine.

C. Study the examples.

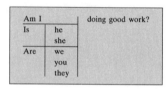

Am I		doing good work?
Is	he	
	she	
Are	we	
	you	
	they	

Yes,	you	are.
No,		aren't.

What	are you	doing?
Where		going?

36

Unit 3

PREPARATION

If necessary, review the vocabulary in the language boxes with students before they open their books.

PRESENTATION

A. Have students read the language boxes independently. Have students use the words in the language boxes to say as many sentences as they can. Explain to students that they can refer to the language boxes throughout the unit to check or review sentence patterns.

B. Demonstrate by writing the first item on the board. Have students complete the activity. Have several students read the questions and answers aloud.

C. Follow the procedure in A.

D. Miguel and Sylvia are talking on the telephone. Complete the dialog. Use the patterns in A and C.

➤ What _____are_____ you _____doing_____ **(do)?**

● I'm _____studying_____ **(study).**

➤ What _____are_____ you _____studying_____ **(study)?**

● English.

➤ _____Are_____ you _____reading_____ **(read)?**

● No, I'm not. _____I'm writing_____ **(write).**

E. Work with a small group. Use the patterns in A and C to talk about the students in your class.

F. Study the examples.

the student's book   the students' books

G. Write the word. Use 's or s'.

➤ I'm going to the _____counselors'_____ **(counselors)** office.

● Where is it?

➤ It's next to the _____director's_____ **(director)** office.

● Oh. Thanks.

PRESENTATION

D. Follow the procedure in B.

 E. Demonstrate by pantomiming an action and asking students about what you are doing. Then have small groups complete the activity. Have students form new groups and repeat the activity. Ask several groups to present their pantomimes and dialogs to the class.

F. Remind students that the apostrophe precedes the **s** in a singular possessive and follows the **s** in a plural possessive. Give one or two examples.

G. Demonstrate by doing the first item on the board. Then have students complete the activity independently. Have two students read the sentences aloud as the rest of the class checks their answers.

WORKBOOK

Unit 3, Pages 21–22, Exercises 7A–7C.

FOLLOW-UP

Vocabulary Bingo: Have students make a nine-square bingo grid on a piece of paper. If necessary, draw one on the board for them to copy. Write these verbs on the board and have them put them in any square they like: **do, meet, sharpen, write, read, erase, go, open, talk.**

do	write	sharpen
meet	talk	open
erase	read	go

Say a verb and call on a student to use it in a sentence (either a question or a statement). Then have all students mark the verb on their grids with a coin or a piece of paper until someone gets a bingo. Explain that a bingo occurs when a student has three verbs marked in a row horizontally, vertically, or diagonally, and that the first person to get one and say "bingo" aloud wins.

♦ Have students write their sentences on the board when they play the game instead of saying them aloud.

Write It Down

A. Look and read.

Alma's sick.
She's staying home from school.
Ms. Vargas is writing a note to Alma's teacher.

B. Complete the note.

| excuse | home | school | sick |

Dear Mr. Reyna,

Alma is ___sick___ today, Tuesday, January 12.

She's staying ___home___ from ___school___.

Please ___excuse___ her.

Thank you very much.

Ms. Vargas

About You **C. You're sick.**
You're not going to English class today.
Write a note to your teacher on a sheet of paper.

PREPARATION

If necessary, review the vocabulary. Provide any reinforcement necessary. See "Reinforcing Vocabulary" on page vi.

PRESENTATION

Culture Note: You might remind students that in the U.S., schoolchildren are required to attend school on every school day. If they are absent, a note from home explaining the reason for the absence and signed by a parent or guardian is required.

A. Have students read the information with the picture and talk about it. Encourage them to say everything they can about it. Write their ideas on the board or restate them in acceptable English. Point out the important elements that should be included in an absentee note: the teacher's name, the reason for the absence, and the signature of the parent.

B. Have students complete the activity independently. Ask several students to read their notes aloud while the other students check their own answers.

About You C. Have students write notes to you, using the proper form. Have volunteers share their notes with the class.

WORKBOOK

Unit 3, Page 22, Exercise 8.

FOLLOW-UP

A Note to the Teacher: Write three or four situations in which a parent needs to write an absentee note, such as a stomachache, headache, broken arm, etc., on sheets of paper. Divide the class into small groups and give each group one of the situations. Have group members work together to write an absentee note about an imaginary child. Then have each group choose one student to read the note to the rest of the class.

♦ Have students brainstorm a list of valid reasons for being absent from school (stomachache, headache, broken arm). Write the list on the board. Have each student choose a reason from the list and write an absentee note about an imaginary child. Have volunteers share their notes with the class.

One To One
Student A

I. Practice the dialog.

➤ Excuse me. Where's the **library?**
● **Go down the hall. Turn left. The library's on the right.**
➤ OK. Thanks.
● You're welcome.

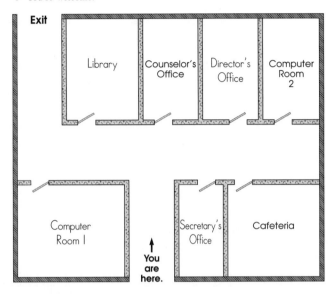

 **2. Ask Student B for directions. Follow the dialog in I.
Write the places on the map.**

the library
the director's office
computer room 1
the secretary's office

 **3. Give Student B directions. Use the map.
Follow the dialog in I.**

4. Switch roles. Turn to page 40. Complete 2 and 3.

Unit 3   39

PREPARATION

If necessary, review names of people
and places at school, location words,
and the language used in asking for
and giving directions. Follow the
instructions in "Preparation" on
page 32.

PRESENTATION

Teaching Note: For more information on these pages, see "One to
One" on page vii.

1. Have students find partners.
Assign the roles of A and B. Explain
that Student A looks only at page A
(page 39) and Student B only at page
B (page 40). Have them turn to the
appropriate pages. Have students
talk about the map. Have everyone

locate the starting point. Then present the dialog. See "Presenting
Dialogs" on page vi.

2. Have students read the
directions independently.
Model the activity with a student.
Then have students complete the
activity.

3. Have students read the
directions independently and
complete the activity.

4. Have students read the directions
and complete the activity. You may
want to have students switch partners at this time, too. Then check
students' answers for both pages.

WORKBOOK

Unit 3, Page 23, Exercise 9.

FOLLOW-UP

Room Names and Locations: On the
board, draw a map of an imaginary
school. Put a starting point on the
map. Decide what each room will be,
but don't label them or tell students.
Make a list of the rooms in the
school beside the map and have students find each room on the list by
asking you questions about the map.
For example, a student might say,
*We want to go to the library. Do we
go right or left inside the front door?*
As you respond to each question,
invite a different student to ask the
next one. As each room is located,
mark it off the list.

♦ Give pairs of students written
directions to each room on the map.
Ask partners to find and label the
rooms.

Identify people and places at school

Talk about where places are in
  buildings

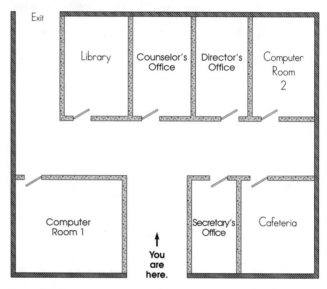

One To One   **Student B**

I. Practice the dialog.

➤ Excuse me. Where's the **library**?
● Go down the hall. Turn left. The library's on the right.
➤ OK. Thanks.
● You're welcome.

2. Give Student A directions. Use the map.
Follow the dialog in I.

3. Ask Student A for directions. Follow the dialog in I.
Write the places on the map.

computer room 2
the cafeteria
the exit

4. Switch roles. Turn to page 39. Complete 2 and 3.

40   Unit 3

PRESENTATION

Follow the instructions on page 39.

Extension

A. Look at the building directory and the map.

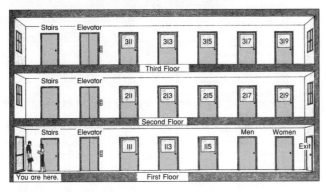

 B. Practice the dialog.

> ➤ Excuse me. Where's the **Level 1 English class?**
> ● On the **third floor,** room **317.**
> ➤ How do I get there?
> ● **Go up the stairs or take the elevator to the third floor.**
>   **Then go down the hall.**
> ➤ OK. Thanks.
> ● You're welcome.

C. Work with a partner.
Use the building directory and the map.
Where do you want to go? Use the dialog in B.

C. Demonstrate by having a student ask you questions similar to those in B. Have pairs of students use the directory and the map to complete the activity. Ask pairs of students to present their dialogs for the class.

WORKBOOK

Unit 3, Page 24, Exercise 10.

FOLLOW-UP

The New Student: Make copies of a simple directory for the building where your class is held. Have students work in pairs, one acting as a new student in their school and the other as a student who is helping the newcomer find a classroom. Remind students to use floor and room numbers in their directions. Have volunteers present their conversations to the class.

◆ Have students write a sentence or two telling a new student how to get to their classroom from the front entrance of the building. Remind them to include the room and floor numbers.

PREPARATION

Preteach or review the new vocabulary. Follow these suggestions.

● If your classroom building has a directory, you may want to take the class to look at it. Teach pertinent language, such as **stairs, elevator,** and **go up.**

Teaching Note: Remind students that the first number in a room number usually corresponds to the floor the room is on; for instance, **317** indicates a room on the third floor.

You might want to point out to students the differences in the meanings of the words **up** and **down** when they are used in the phrases **up** (or **down**) **the hall** and **up** (or **down**) **the stairs.**

Culture Note: You might mention that in the U.S., what is called the first floor is almost always the ground floor; in many countries, the first floor is the first one above the ground floor.

PRESENTATION

A. Have students preview the directory and the map. Encourage them to say everything they can about them. Write their ideas on the board or restate them in acceptable English. Have students read the directory and look at the map independently.

B. Present the dialog. See "Presenting Dialogs" on page vi. Remind students to use the directory and the map.

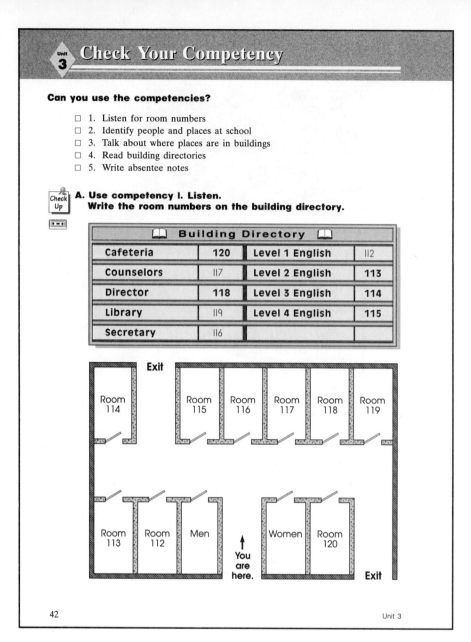

Can you use the competencies?

☐ 1. Listen for room numbers
☐ 2. Identify people and places at school
☐ 3. Talk about where places are in buildings
☐ 4. Read building directories
☐ 5. Write absentee notes

Check Up

**A. Use competency I. Listen.
Write the room numbers on the building directory.**

📖 Building Directory 📖			
Cafeteria	120	Level 1 English	II2
Counselors	II7	Level 2 English	113
Director	118	Level 3 English	114
Library	II9	Level 4 English	115
Secretary	II6		

Exit

Room 114

Room 115 | Room 116 | Room 117 | Room 118 | Room 119

Room 113 | Room 112 | Men

↑
You are here.

Women | Room 120

Exit

42

Unit 3

PRESENTATION

Use any of the procedures in "Evaluation," page viii, with these pages. For Exercise A, play the tape or read the Listening Transcript aloud two or more times. Record individuals' results on the Unit 3 Individual Competency Chart. Record the class's results on the Class Cumulative Competency Chart.

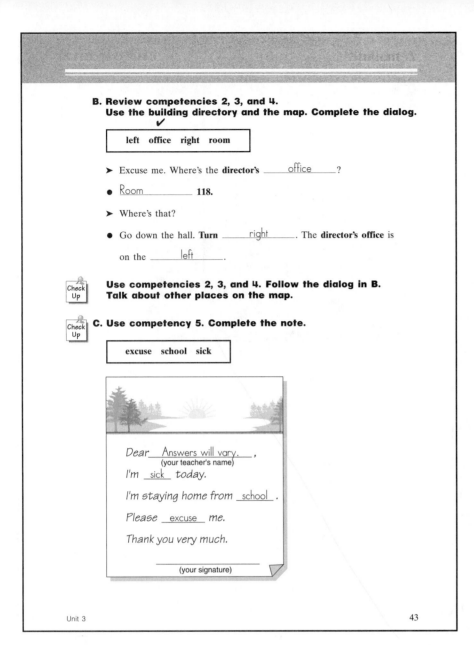

B. Review competencies 2, 3, and 4.
   Use the building directory and the map. Complete the dialog.

| left office right room |

➤ Excuse me. Where's the **director's** ___office___ ?

● ___Room___ **118.**

➤ Where's that?

● Go down the hall. **Turn** ___right___ . The **director's office** is

   on the ___left___ .

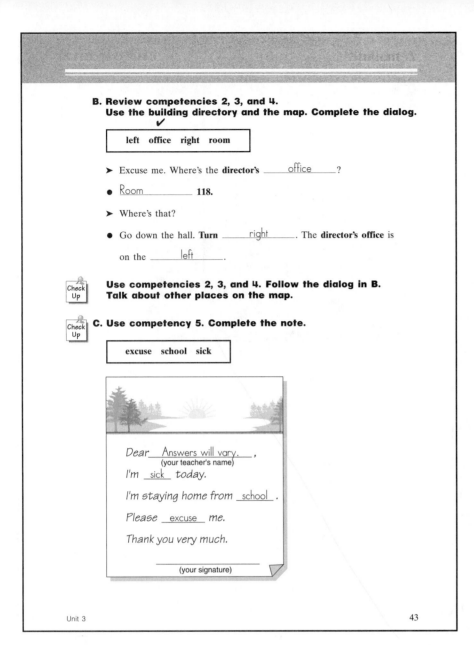 **Use competencies 2, 3, and 4. Follow the dialog in B.**
   Talk about other places on the map.

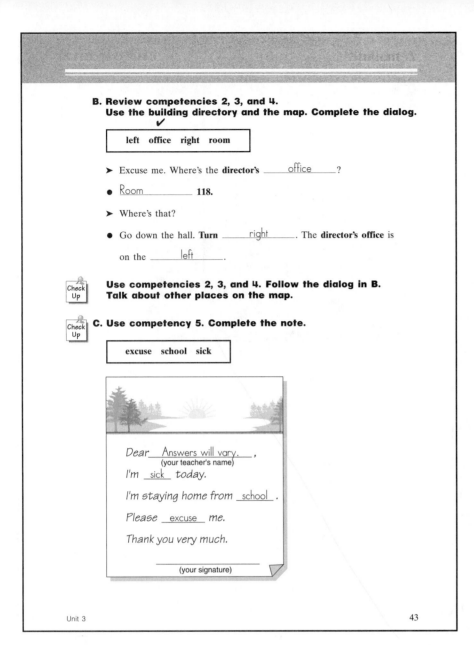 **C. Use competency 5. Complete the note.**

| excuse school sick |

Dear ___Answers will vary.___ ,
        (your teacher's name)
I'm ___sick___ today.

I'm staying home from ___school___ .

Please ___excuse___ me.

Thank you very much.

_____
        (your signature)

Unit 3   43

FOLLOW-UP

ENGLISH IN ACTION

An Optional Cooperative Learning Project: You may want to have students work together to prepare a newcomer's guide to an elementary, middle, or high school in the area. It might contain a map of the school building and all the pertinent information about the school. Help students make a list of items they want to include. Suggest that a directory of names and room numbers of school personnel be included. Make sure they include the names of the people in charge of ESL programs. Help students organize and compile the information into a booklet. Make more than one copy if possible. Have new students use the guide and tell the class how it helped them.

Unit 4 Overview

UNIT WARM-UP

The focus of Unit 4, "Daily Living," is talking and writing about the weather, the seasons of the year, and times and dates. To stimulate a discussion, hold up several pictures depicting different types of weather. Have students say whether the weather is good or bad and ask them to explain their answers as best they can. Ask students, *When is it important to talk about the weather? When is it important to talk about the time? the day? the date? When do you write the date?*

Unit 4 Optional Materials

● Simple picture cards or photographs of the seasons and weather types (rain, snow, wind, sunshine).

● A large calendar.

● A simple clock with movable hands.

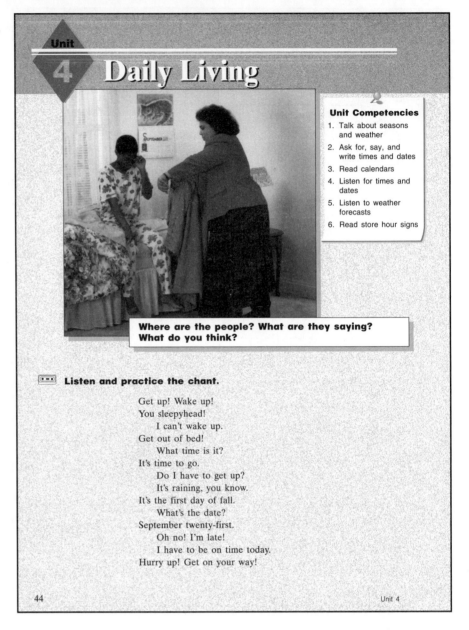

Unit 4 **Daily Living**

Unit Competencies

1. Talk about seasons and weather
2. Ask for, say, and write times and dates
3. Read calendars
4. Listen for times and dates
5. Listen to weather forecasts
6. Read store hour signs

Where are the people? What are they saying? What do you think?

Listen and practice the chant.

Get up! Wake up!
You sleepyhead!
 I can't wake up.
Get out of bed!
 What time is it?
It's time to go.
 Do I have to get up?
 It's raining, you know.
It's the first day of fall.
 What's the date?
September twenty-first.
 Oh no! I'm late!
 I have to be on time today.
Hurry up! Get on your way!

44   Unit 4

COMPETENCIES (page 44)

Talk about seasons and weather

Ask for, say, and write times and dates

PREPARATION

Use pantomime, the picture cards or photographs, and the large calendar to preteach the new language in the chant. Follow these suggestions.

● Hold up each picture card or photograph and name the weather or season to present **raining** and **fall.** To present the date, use the large calendar to point out September twenty-first. Have students repeat each one after you.

● You may also want to preteach other expressions in the chant: **Get**
up! Wake up! You sleepyhead!
Hurry up! Get on your way!

PRESENTATION

Focus attention on the photo and have students answer the questions. Encourage them to say everything they can about it. Write their ideas on the board or restate them in acceptable English.

Present the chant. See "Presenting Chants" on page vi.

WORKBOOK

Unit 4, Page 25, Exercise 1.

FOLLOW-UP

Get Up, Sleepyhead! Have students say the chant in pairs, each student

taking one part. Have them use body language and gestures. Have volunteers present their role-plays in front of the class.

♦ Have students work in pairs. Ask them to recall times when they were late for appointments. Have students tell their partners' stories to the class.

Starting Out

A. Look, listen, and read.

1. It's January 3. It's winter.
   It's a cold night.
   It's snowing. It's very windy.
   She's driving home.

2. It's April 9. It's spring.
   It's a warm morning.
   It's raining.
   She's walking to work.

3. It's July 19. It's summer.
   It's a hot afternoon.
   It's very sunny.
   He's cutting the grass at work.

4. It's October 30. It's fall.
   It's a cool morning.
   It's cloudy.
   They're going to school.

**B. Work with a partner.
Answer the questions.**

1. It's summer. How's the weather?
2. It's winter. How's the weather?
3. It's spring. How's the weather?

 **C. Work with a partner.
Use the sentences in A to talk about the weather today.
What are people doing?**

Unit 4   45

PREPARATION

Use the picture cards or photographs of the seasons and the weather, and the large calendar to preteach the new language. Follow these suggestions.

● To present the seasons and weather, hold up picture cards or photos depicting each one. Say, *It's (spring, fall,* etc.). *It's hot (cold,* etc.). Have students repeat.

● To present dates, use the large calendar to point out months and dates. Say, *It's April 9 (July 19,* etc.).

● Call attention to the time of day (morning, afternoon, or night) depicted in each photo. Model, *It's morning (afternoon,* etc.). Have students repeat.

PRESENTATION

A. Have students talk about the photographs. Encourage them to say everything they can about them. Write their ideas on the board or restate them in acceptable English. Then play the tape or read the captions aloud as students follow along in their books. Have students read the captions again independently.

B. Demonstrate by writing the first item on the board. Have students complete the activity. Ask several students to say their answers aloud.

C. Demonstrate by making statements about the seasons, the weather, and seasonal activities to a student. Have students complete the activity. Then have students switch partners and repeat. Have

several pairs present their dialogs to the class.

WORKBOOK

Unit 4, Page 26, Exercise 2.

FOLLOW-UP

Weather Report: Have pairs of students use your pictures or photographs to talk about the weather. Have partners take turns asking about the weather and describing it. Have several pairs present their conversations to the class.

◆ Divide the class into small groups. Have each group choose a season and a time of day. Have them write a few sentences describing the weather and what people might be doing. Have one member of each group read their sentences to the class.

Talk It Over

A. Listen and practice the dialogs.

➤ What time is it?
● It's **two o'clock**.
➤ **Two o'clock?**
● Yes.
➤ Thanks.

➤ What time is it?
● It's **three-thirty**.
➤ Excuse me?
● **Three-thirty**.
➤ Thanks.

B. Write the times.

12:00

9:15

7:30

2:45

C. Work with a partner. Follow one of the dialogs in A.
    Say the times in B.

D. Ask your partner the time.
    Follow one of the dialogs in A.

46   Unit 4

PREPARATION

Use the clock or draw a clock face on the board to preteach saying the time in English. Set the clock to various hours and model saying the times, *It's (four) o'clock.* Continue with hours and minutes, *It's four-fifteen.*

PRESENTATION

A. Have students talk about the pictures. Encourage them to say everything they can about them. Write their ideas on the board or restate them in acceptable English. Then present the dialogs. See "Presenting Dialogs" on page vi.

B. Demonstrate by writing the first item on the board. Have students complete the activity independently. Ask several students to

say the times while the rest of the class checks their own answers.

C. Demonstrate by having a student ask you the questions in A. Use the picture of the first clock in B to answer. Have students complete the activity. Then have students switch partners and repeat the activity. Ask several pairs to present their dialogs to the class.

D. Demonstrate by asking a student the time. Have students complete the activity. Then have students switch partners and repeat the activity. Ask several pairs to present their dialogs to the class.

WORKBOOK

Unit 4, Page 27, Exercise 3.

FOLLOW-UP

What Time Is It? Have students use the clock or a clock face drawn on the board. Have three students come to the front of the class. Have one student set the clock to a certain time. Ask the other two students to make up a dialog similar to A about the time the clock shows.

◆ Ask students to imagine that it's various times and say what they're doing. Say, *It's (two) o'clock. What are you doing?*

Word Bank

A. Study the vocabulary.

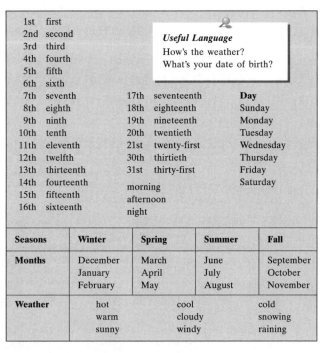

1st	first
2nd	second
3rd	third
4th	fourth
5th	fifth
6th	sixth

Useful Language
How's the weather?
What's your date of birth?

7th	seventh	17th	seventeenth	**Day**
8th	eighth	18th	eighteenth	Sunday
9th	ninth	19th	nineteenth	Monday
10th	tenth	20th	twentieth	Tuesday
11th	eleventh	21st	twenty-first	Wednesday
12th	twelfth	30th	thirtieth	Thursday
13th	thirteenth	31st	thirty-first	Friday
14th	fourteenth			Saturday
15th	fifteenth	morning		
16th	sixteenth	afternoon		
		night		

Seasons	Winter	Spring	Summer	Fall
Months	December January February	March April May	June July August	September October November
Weather	hot warm sunny	cool cloudy windy		cold snowing raining

B. Look and read.

We write: _____ July 12, 1994 _____ .

We say: _____ July twelfth, nineteen ninety-four _____ .

 C. Work with a partner. Say the dates.

1. November 2, 1995   2. July 13, 1997
3. February 23, 1996   4. October 31, 1994

PREPARATION

Preteach or review the new vocabulary before students open their books. Give special attention to the ordinal numbers. Use the large calendar to review or introduce the days of the week, the months of the year, and the meanings of **today** and **tomorrow.** Review or introduce the times of day, seasons, and weather words. Provide any reinforcement necessary. See "Reinforcing Vocabulary" on page vi.

PRESENTATION

A. Have students scan the list. Define, or have other students define, any words individuals do not recognize. Provide any reinforcement necessary. See "Reinforcing Vocabulary" on page vi. Remind students that they can use this list throughout the unit to look up words, to check spelling, and to find key phrases.

Teaching Note: You might present the expressions **a quarter past, half past,** and **a quarter to.** You also might present **midnight, noon, A.M., and P.M.**

B. Demonstrate by writing a date on the board and then saying the date. Have students repeat. Have several students read the date on the page to the class.

C. Demonstrate by saying the first date to a student. Have pairs complete the activity. Have students switch partners and repeat the activity. Have several pairs present their dialogs to the class.

WORKBOOK

Unit 4, Pages 27–28, Exercises 4A–4C.

FOLLOW-UP

Special Dates: Have students work in pairs. Ask them to talk about special dates in their lives, such as birthdays, the birthdays of their children or grandchildren, anniversaries, the day they arrived in the U.S., etc. Have partners tell the rest of the class about each other's special dates.

♦ Have students write down three special dates in their lives and then write a sentence about each one. Have volunteers share their work with the class.

COMPETENCIES (page 48)

Talk about seasons and weather

Ask for, say, and write times and dates

Read calendars

Listen for times and dates

Listen to weather forecasts

Listening

 A. Look, listen, and write the time.

1. _____9:00_____
2. _____10:45_____
3. _____12:15_____
4. _____5:30_____

 B. Look, listen, and circle the date.

1. (June 7)   June 17   June 27
2. October 6   October 16   (October 26)
3. April 9   (April 19)   April 29

 C. Look and listen to the weather forecast.
Write the number of the forecast on the line.

_____1_____   _____2_____

48   Unit 4

PREPARATION

If necessary, review the names of the months of the year and the language used for talking about time and weather. Use the weather and season photos or picture cards, the clock, and the large calendar. Provide any reinforcement necessary. See "Reinforcing Vocabulary" on page vi.

PRESENTATION

A and **B.** Have students complete the activities as you play the tape or read the Listening Transcript aloud two or more times. Make sure students understand they will circle the date they hear in B. Check students' work.

Language Note: You might tell students that English speakers may say *the 23rd of June* instead of *June 23rd.*

C. Have students read the directions. Make sure students understand that they will match the numbers of the forecasts with the pictures. Have students complete the activity as you play the tape or read the Listening Transcript aloud two or more times. Check students' work.

WORKBOOK

Unit 4, Page 29, Exercise 5.

FOLLOW-UP

Date Dictation: Dictate five or six times and dates to students. Have them write their answers on sheets of paper.

♦ Have students work in small groups. Ask each student to write a list of two or three times and dates. Then have students take turns dictating their lists to the other members of the group. Have students compare papers in pairs. Then check everyone's work.

Reading

A. Read the holiday schedule.

SP

Smith Plastics Co.

HOLIDAYS

January 1	New Year's Day
January 18	Martin Luther King Day
February 22	Presidents' Day

B. Circle the holidays on the calendar pages.

January						
S	M	T	W	T	F	S
					①	2
3	4	5	6	7	8	9
10	11	12	13	14	15	16
17	⑱	19	20	21	22	23
24/31	25	26	27	28	29	30

February						
S	M	T	W	T	F	S
1	2	3	4	5	6	
7	8	9	10	11	12	13
14	15	16	17	18	19	20
21	㉒	23	24	25	26	27
28						

C. Complete the sentences about the calendar pages.

1. What day is January 1? It's _____Friday_____.

2. What day is January 18? It's _____Monday_____.

3. What day is February 22? It's _____Monday_____.

D. Work with a partner.
What holidays are coming up? When are they?

Ask for, say, and write times
   and dates

Read calendars

PREPARATION

If necessary, use the large calendar to review the names of the months of the year and the days of the week. Discuss the meaning of **holiday.**

PRESENTATION

A. Have students preview the holiday list for a few minutes before they read it. See "Prereading" on page vii. Encourage them to say everything they can about the list. Write their ideas on the board or restate them in acceptable English.

B. Have students preview the calendars independently. Then have them circle the dates from the holiday list in A. Have several students read their answers aloud while the rest of the class checks their own answers.

C. Demonstrate by asking a student the first question. Have students complete the activity independently. Have students read their answers aloud while the rest of the class checks their own answers.

D. Demonstrate by naming an upcoming holiday and saying when it occurs. Have students complete the activity. Have pairs name the holidays they thought of for the class.

WORKBOOK

Unit 4, Page 29, Exercise 6.

FOLLOW-UP

Holidays: Have small groups of students talk about the traditions associated with holidays in their native countries. Ask them to find similarities in the ways holidays are celebrated in many parts of the world (special foods, certain ceremonies, family gatherings, and so on). Ask groups to report to the class. Write down a list of similarities on the board.

♦ Ask students to choose one holiday, either from their own culture or U.S. culture, and write two or three sentences about it.

Talk about seasons and weather

Ask for, say, and write times
  and dates

Read calendars

Structure Base

A. Study the examples.

What	month	is it?
	day	
	season	
	time	

It's	May.
	Tuesday.
	spring.
	10:00.

B. Look at the picture.
   Answer the questions.
   Use the words in A.

1. What month is it? _____ It's April.

2. What day is it? _____ It's Saturday.

3. What time is it? _____ It's 11:15.

C. Study the examples.

| It's | raining. |
| | snowing. |

It's	sunny.
	cold.
	windy.
	cool.
	hot.

D. Work with a partner.
   Talk about the time, the date, and the weather.
   Use the words in A and C.

50   Unit 4

PREPARATION

If necessary, review the vocabulary in the language boxes with students before they open their books. Follow the instructions in "Preparation" on page 48.

PRESENTATION

A. Have students read the language boxes independently. Have students use the words in the language boxes to say as many sentences as they can. Explain to students that they can refer to the language boxes throughout the unit to check or review sentence patterns.

B. Demonstrate by writing the first item on the board. Have students complete the activity. Have several students read the questions and answers aloud.

C. Follow the procedure in A.

D. Demonstrate by telling a student about the time, the date, and the weather. Have students complete the activity. Have several pairs present their dialogs to the class.

E. Study the examples.

Is it	snowing?
	cold?
	January?
	winter?
	sunny?
	Saturday?

Yes,	it	is.
No,		isn't.

F. Look at the picture.
Complete the sentences.
Use the words from E.

1. _____Is it_____ **December?**   No, ____it isn't____ .

2. _____Is it_____ **January?**   Yes, ____it is____ .

3. _____Is it_____ **warm?**   No, ____it isn't____ .

4. _____Is it_____ **cold?**   Yes, ____it is____ .

5. _____Is it_____ **snowing?**   Yes, ____it is____ .

 G. Work with a partner.
Talk about the weather today.
Follow the sentences in F.

PRESENTATION

E. Follow the procedure in A.

F. Demonstrate by completing the first item on the board. Have students complete the activity. Have several students read the sentences aloud.

 G. Demonstrate by asking a student the questions in F. Help the student answer. Have students complete the activity. Have several pairs present their dialogs to the class.

WORKBOOK

Unit 4, Pages 30–31, Exercises 7A–7C.

FOLLOW-UP

Draw this simple schedule on the board. Have students copy it onto sheets of paper and complete it about a typical day. (Encourage students to change the hours to match their routines.) Have volunteers show their schedules to the class and talk about them.

Time	Activity
8:00 A.M.	
9:00	
10:00	
11:00	
12:00 P.M.	
1:00	

♦ Have students work in pairs and complete schedules for their partners.

Write It Down

**A. Kwan's date of birth is April 12, 1970.
He wrote his date of birth on the form.
Look and read.**

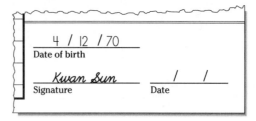

4 / 12 / 70
Date of birth

Kwan Sun   / /
Signature   Date

B. Study the chart.

1	=	January	7	=	July	55	=	1955
2	=	February	8	=	August	60	=	1960
3	=	March	9	=	September	65	=	1965
4	=	April	10	=	October	70	=	1970
5	=	May	11	=	November	71	=	1971
6	=	June	12	=	December	72	=	1972

C. Write today's date on the form in A.

 D. Write today's date and your date of birth on the form.

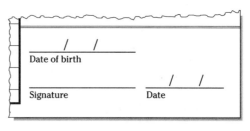

/ /
Date of birth

_____   / /
Signature   Date

52   Unit 4

PREPARATION

If necessary, review the names of the months of the year. Introduce the numerical representation of the months of the year. Say, *January is the first month, so January second is 1/2.* Tell students that in the U.S., dates are written numerically by month, day, and year. December 5, 1994, is written **12/5/94.**

PRESENTATION

A. Have students talk about the form. Encourage them to say everything they can about it. Ask them to say how the date is written.

Language Note: Tell students that birthdates include months, days, and years. Birthdays include only months and days.

B. Have students look at the chart. Then ask one student to say the number of a month and another student to name the corresponding month until everyone has had a chance to participate.

C. Have students complete the activity independently. Ask students to read their answers aloud.

D. Demonstrate by drawing a simple form on the board and writing the date and your birth date (or any other logical date) in the appropriate places. Have students complete the activity.

Culture Note: You might warn students that some English speakers do not like to talk about their ages or years of birth. It is, however, accept-

able to ask about someone's birthday.

WORKBOOK

Unit 4, Page 31, Exercise 8.

FOLLOW-UP

Birthdays: Have students compile a class birthday list. Ask them to write their names and birthdays in a column on the board. Remind them to use the numerical style presented on this page. Have the class help you write a new list on the board, ordering the birthdays by month.

♦ Have students make a list of their family members and their birthdays. Remind them to use the style presented on this page and to write the dates in order by month.

One To One — Student A

I. Practice the dialog.

- ➤ Excuse me. What's the **date?**
- ● **November 27.**
- ➤ What **time** is it?
- ● It's **4:30.**
- ➤ Excuse me?
- ● **4:30.**

2. Ask Student B for the time and the date.
Follow the dialog in I. Write the information.

a. _____November 27_____
_____4:30_____

b. _____January 15_____
_____2:00_____

c. _____September 20_____
_____6:15_____

3. Give Student B the time and the date. Follow the dialog in I.

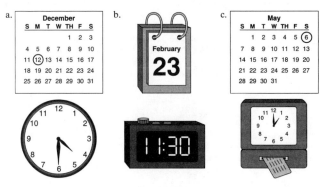

4. Switch roles. Turn to page 54. Complete 2 and 3.

PREPARATION

If necessary, review names of the months of the year and the language used for talking about time. Follow any of the suggestions in Preparation on pages 45–49.

PRESENTATION

Teaching Note: For more information on these pages, see "One to One" on page vii.

1. Have students find partners. Assign the roles of A and B. Explain that Student A looks only at page A (page 53) and Student B only at page B (page 54). Have them turn to the appropriate page. Have students look at the calendar and the clock. Then present the dialog. See "Presenting Dialogs" on page vi.

2. Have students read the directions independently. Model the activity with a student. Then have the students complete the activity.

3. Have students read the directions independently and complete the activity.

4. Have students read the directions and complete the activity. You may want students to switch partners at this time, too. Check students' answers for both pages.

WORKBOOK

Unit 4, Page 32, Exercise 9.

FOLLOW-UP

What's the Date? Provide students with newspaper ads for movies, concerts, and other events. Have pairs of students work on skits. Have partners plan to attend an event and ask each other questions about dates and times. Remind them to use the clarification strategy of asking *Excuse me?* to request repetition. Invite partners to present their skits to the class.

♦ Have students write ads for any event they choose. Remind them to include the time, the date, and the place. Post their ads around the room.

One To One

Student B

I. Practice the dialog.

> ➤ Excuse me. What's the **date?**
> ● **November 27.**
> ➤ What **time** is it?
> ● It's **4:30.**
> ➤ Excuse me?
> ● **4:30.**

 2. Give Student A the time and the date. Follow the dialog in I.

a.

b.

c.

 3. Ask Student A for the time and the date.
Follow the dialog in I. Write the information.

a. ___December 12___
___4:30___

b. ___February 23___
___11:30___

c. ___May 6___
___1:00___

4. Switch roles. Turn to page 53. Complete 2 and 3.

PRESENTATION

Follow the instructions on page 53.

Extension

BANK HOURS
MONDAY–FRIDAY 8:00–5:00
SATURDAY 9:00–12:00

*We will close at 3:00
on New Year's Eve.
We will reopen
Saturday, January 2.
Happy New Year!*

 A. Practice the dialog.

➤ Are you open tomorrow?
● Yes. But we close early. It's New Year's Eve.
➤ What about Friday?
● It's New Year's Day. We're closed all day.
➤ When do you open?
● On Saturday.
➤ What are the hours?
● 9 o'clock to 12 noon.

 B. Work with a partner.
Answer the questions.

1. What time does the bank close on New Year's Eve?
2. Is the bank open on Friday?
3. What time does the bank open on Saturday?

COMPETENCIES (page 55)
Ask for and say times and dates
Read store hour signs

PREPARATION

● Hold up a picture of a bank and explain the duties of a bank guard. If necessary, discuss the meanings of the words **open, closed,** and **reopen.**

● Clarify the New Year's Eve holiday, if necessary, and explain that many businesses close early or do not open at all on certain holidays.

PRESENTATION

A. Have students talk about the picture. Encourage them to say everything they can about it. Write their ideas on the board or restate them in acceptable English. Then present the dialog. See "Presenting Dialogs" on page vi.

B. Have students complete the activity in pairs. Then check everyone's answers.

WORKBOOK

Unit 4, Page 32, Exercise 10.

FOLLOW-UP

Open or Closed? Create, or have students create, several business hours signs like the one on this page. Include special notices about holiday closings. Divide the class into small groups and give each group a sign. Have members of the group take turns asking each other questions about their signs, such as, *Can I go to the bank at 6:00 on Friday evening?*

or *Can I take my shoes to the repair shop at 7:15 on Monday morning?*

♦ Post the business hours signs around the room. Have students work in pairs. Give each pair a day of the week and a time of day and ask them to read all the signs and report to the class about what places of business will be open at the assigned day and time.

Can you use the competencies?

- [ ] 1. Talk about seasons and weather
- [ ] 2. Ask for, say, and write times and dates
- [ ] 3. Read calendars
- [ ] 4. Listen for times and dates
- [ ] 5. Listen to weather forecasts
- [ ] 6. Read store hour signs

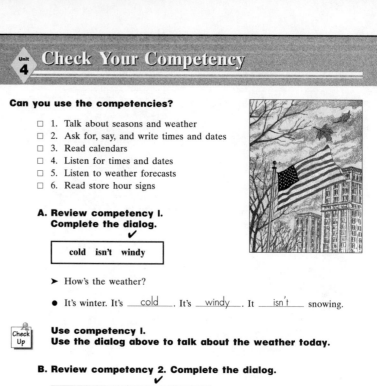

A. Review competency I. Complete the dialog. ✔

| cold   isn't   windy |

➤ How's the weather?

● It's winter. It's __cold__. It's __windy__. It __isn't__ snowing.

Check Up

Use competency I.
Use the dialog above to talk about the weather today.

B. Review competency 2. Complete the dialog. ✔

| date   January 10   me   time |

➤ Excuse ___me___. What's today's ___date___?

● It's ___January 10___.

➤ What ___time___ is it?

● It's **4:00.**

Check Up

Use competency 2.
Use the dialog above to talk about today.
Then write the time and the date.

Today is ___Answers will vary___.

It's ___Answers will vary___.

56

PRESENTATION

Use any of the procedures in "Evaluation," page viii with these pages. For exercise D, play the tape or read the Listening Transcript two or more times. Record individuals' results on the Unit 4 Individual Competency Chart. Record the class's results on the Class Cumulative Competency Chart.

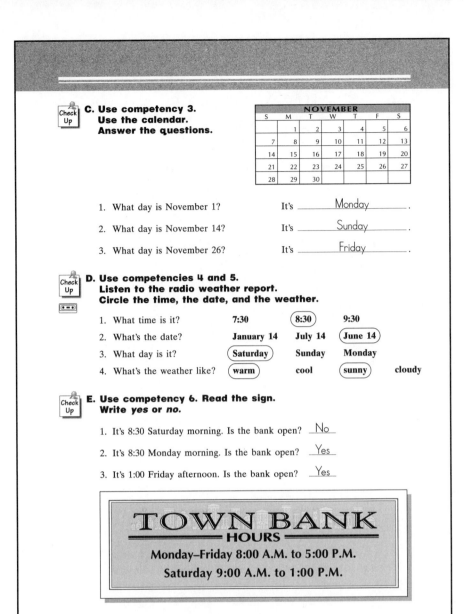

C. Use competency 3.
Use the calendar.
Answer the questions.

NOVEMBER						
S	M	T	W	T	F	S
	1	2	3	4	5	6
7	8	9	10	11	12	13
14	15	16	17	18	19	20
21	22	23	24	25	26	27
28	29	30				

1. What day is November 1?   It's ____Monday____.

2. What day is November 14?   It's ____Sunday____.

3. What day is November 26?   It's ____Friday____.

D. Use competencies 4 and 5.
Listen to the radio weather report.
Circle the time, the date, and the weather.

1. What time is it?   7:30   (8:30)   9:30

2. What's the date?   January 14   July 14   (June 14)

3. What day is it?   (Saturday)   Sunday   Monday

4. What's the weather like?   (warm)   cool   (sunny)   cloudy

E. Use competency 6. Read the sign.
Write *yes* or *no*.

1. It's 8:30 Saturday morning. Is the bank open? _No_

2. It's 8:30 Monday morning. Is the bank open? _Yes_

3. It's 1:00 Friday afternoon. Is the bank open? _Yes_

TOWN BANK
═ HOURS ═
Monday–Friday 8:00 A.M. to 5:00 P.M.
Saturday 9:00 A.M. to 1:00 P.M.

Unit 4   57

FOLLOW-UP

ENGLISH IN ACTION

An Optional Cooperative Learning Project: You may want to have students create a class entertainment guide. Students can interview one another and compile information about their favorite places to go and things to do. Suggest that the guide include the name of each place, the address, the telephone number, a description of what one can do there, how much activities cost, and the hours and days of the week each place is open. For seasonal activities, have students include months and season, too. The guide might be divided into interest sections, such as restaurants, sports, dancing, music, and movies.

Post sheets of paper for the interest sections around the room and ask students to contribute their ideas. Have students proofread and make a final version of each list. Put all the lists in a notebook and suggest that students refer to it when they are looking for things to do.

Unit 5 Overview

UNIT WARM-UP

The focus of Unit 5, "Food," is kinds of food, food packaging, and grocery shopping. To stimulate a discussion, you might arrange several food items and/or packages around the room and role-play shopping for food, first making your list and then commenting as you "shop" on prices and freshness. Encourage students to talk about their own experiences shopping for food.

Unit 5 Optional Materials

- Pictures and/or realia of the food mentioned in this unit (apples, bananas, beans, bread, broccoli, butter, cake, candy, carrots, cheese, chicken, cookies, corn, eggs, fish, grapes, ground beef, jam, lettuce, milk, oil, onions, oranges, pork, potatoes, rice, steak, tea, tomatoes, and watermelon).

- Supermarket circulars. You might ask a supermarket manager for enough copies of the store's circular to give one to each student.

- Various food packages, some with expiration dates.

- A large floor plan of a supermarket interior with the sections labeled (bakery, dairy, meat, and fruits and vegetables) and the aisles numbered.

5 Food

Where are the people? What are they saying? What do you think?

Listen and practice the chant.

Excuse me, please, I'm looking for tea.

It's on the top shelf in aisle three.

What else do we need?

A gallon of milk, two pounds of steak,
A loaf of bread, and a chocolate cake.

Anything else?

Some corn and beans, and strawberry jam.

Ready to check out?

Yes, I am.

58   Unit 5

COMPETENCIES (page 58)

Identify kinds of food

Ask where things are in a supermarket

Listen for aisle numbers

PREPARATION

Use pictures and/or realia, and the supermarket map to preteach the new language in the chant. Follow these suggestions.

- To present **tea, milk, steak, bread, cake, corn, beans, jam, gallon, pound,** and **loaf,** hold up each picture or item and name it. Have students repeat.

- Point out the aisle numbers on the supermarket map.

- You might also preteach the questions in the chant: **What else do we need? Anything else? Ready to check out?**

PRESENTATION

Focus attention on the photo and have students answer the questions. Encourage them to say everything they can about it. Write their ideas on the board or restate them in acceptable English.

Present the chant. See "Presenting Chants" on page vi.

WORKBOOK

Unit 5, Page 33, Exercise 1.

FOLLOW-UP

What Do We Want? Pass out pictures of food to pairs of students. Have them use the pictures to make up conversations in which they ask and answer questions about shopping for the food. Have several pairs present their conversations to the class.

◆ Have pairs write their conversations.

Starting Out

A. Practice the dialogs.

➤ Excuse me. I want **carrots**
  and a **watermelon.**
  Where's the fruit and
  vegetable section?
● Aisle 1.

➤ I want **some bread.**
  Where's the bakery?
● Aisle 2.

➤ I want **a half gallon of milk**
  and **a dozen eggs.**
  Where's the dairy section?
● Aisle 3.

➤ I want **two pounds of chicken**
  and **a pound of ground beef.**
  Where's the meat section?
● Aisle 4.

B. Work with a partner.
Use the dialogs in A to ask where you can find the food.

1. cheese
2. potatoes
3. steak
4. lettuce
5. apples

Unit 5   59

PREPARATION

Use pictures and/or realia, and the
supermarket map to preteach the
new language.

● Use the map to present the sections and aisle numbers in the supermarket. Point to the sections and
name them. Have students say the
names after you. Point out the aisle
numbers.

● Hold up food items or pictures of
food items and have students decide
which section each one belongs in.
Have students name the aisle number for each section.

● Use pictures or containers to
explain **half-gallon, dozen,** and
pound.

PRESENTATION

A. Have students look at the pictures. Encourage students to say
everything they can about them.
Write their ideas on the board or
restate them in acceptable English.
Then present the dialog. See
"Presenting Dialogs" on page vi.

B. Demonstrate by doing the
first item with a student. Have
students complete the activity in
pairs. Then have students switch
partners and repeat the activity. Ask
several pairs of students to present
their dialogs to the class.

WORKBOOK

Unit 5, Page 33, Exercise 2.

FOLLOW-UP

Food Lists: Divide the class into
small groups. Have each group write
the names of the supermarket sections across the top of a piece of
paper and see how many food items
the group can list for each section.
Students might use supermarket circulars to get ideas. Help students
mark out any incorrect choices
before groups compare their papers
to see whose lists are the longest.

◆ Have students work independently
to see how many food items they can
list for each section of the supermarket. Ask students to exchange papers
and check each other's work. Then
see whose lists are the longest.

Talk It Over

 A. Practice the dialog.

> ➤ What do we want from the grocery store, Bill?
> ● **Apples, oranges, and bananas.**
> ➤ Anything else?
> ● **Some cheese.**
> ➤ How much?
> ● About **half a pound.**
> ➤ Is that all?
> ● No. Let's get **a bottle of oil and a loaf of bread,** too.
> ➤ OK.

About You **B. Work with three other students.**
Talk about what they want from the grocery store.
Write the answers.

Name	Food
Bill	apples, oranges, bananas, cheese, oil, bread

60   Unit 5

PREPARATION

Use pictures and/or realia to preteach the new language. Follow these suggestions.

● Review the names of the food used on this page, if necessary. Review the meanings of **pound** and **loaf,** if necessary.

PRESENTATION

A. Have students talk about the photo. Encourage them to say everything they can about it. Write their ideas on the board or restate them in acceptable English. Then present the dialog. See "Presenting Dialogs" on page vi.

About You **B.** Demonstrate by making a chart like the one in B on the board. Ask a student what groceries

he or she wants and write the answers on your chart. Have students work in groups of four to complete the activity. Ask several students to read their lists aloud to the class.

WORKBOOK

Unit 5, Page 34, Exercise 3.

FOLLOW-UP

Food Purchases: Have students write down the three or four food items they purchase most frequently. As they read their lists aloud, write the name of each food on the board and add a check mark each time an item is repeated. Have students tally up the check marks to see which food items are purchased frequently by

several members of the class.

♦ Have students look at the list on the board and talk about why they think certain food items are purchased more frequently than others.

Identify kinds of food
Write shopping lists

Word Bank

A. Study the vocabulary.

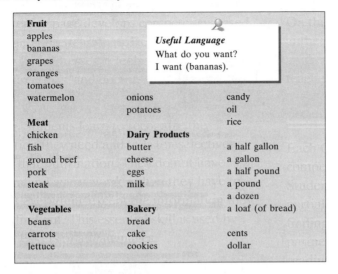

Fruit
apples
bananas
grapes
oranges
tomatoes
watermelon

Useful Language
What do you want?
I want (bananas).

onions   candy
potatoes   oil
                rice

Meat
chicken   **Dairy Products**
fish   butter   a half gallon
ground beef   cheese   a gallon
pork   eggs   a half pound
steak   milk   a pound
                                a dozen

Vegetables   **Bakery**   a loaf (of bread)
beans   bread
carrots   cake   cents
lettuce   cookies   dollar

B. Look at the pictures. What are they?
Where do you find them? Write the section.

Food	Section
grapes	fruit and vegetable
cookies	bakery
butter	dairy
carrots	fruit and vegetable
fish	meat

C. Work with a partner. Look at the food in B.
What do you want? Write a list of food on a sheet of paper.
Write the sections where you find them.

Unit 5   61

of students to present their answers to the class.

PREPARATION

Use pictures and/or realia, and packages to preteach or review the new vocabulary before students open their books. Give special attention to **grapes, onions, tomatoes, butter, fish, ground beef,** and **rice;** quantity words; and **cents** and **dollar.** Provide any reinforcement necessary. See "Reinforcing Vocabulary" on page vi.

PRESENTATION

A. Have students scan the list. Define, or have students define, any words individuals do not recognize. Provide any reinforcement necessary. See "Reinforcing Vocabulary" on page vi. Remind students that they can use this list throughout the unit to look up words, to check spelling, and to find key phrases.

B. Have students look back at the pictures. Encourage students to say everything they can about them. Make sure students understand that they should use the names of the food in the pictures and the supermarket section each is found in to complete the exercise. Have students complete the activity independently. Have several students read their answers aloud while other students check their own answers.

C. Demonstrate by finishing B with foods you like and writing the sections they are found in. Have students complete the activity. Then have students find a partner and share information. Ask several pairs

WORKBOOK

Unit 5, Pages 34–35, Exercises 4A–4C.

FOLLOW-UP

Shopping List: Use the supermarket map and a shopping list that includes food from each section of the store. Have students work in pairs. Give each pair a copy of the shopping list and ask them to use the map to organize the list by sections, starting with the section in aisle 1. Have each pair share their new list with the rest of the class.

♦ Have pairs of students write shopping lists for other pairs to organize by supermarket section. Have several pairs post their organized lists for the rest of the class to read.

Identify kinds of food

Write shopping lists

Ask where things are in a supermarket

Listen for aisle numbers

Listening

**A. What are the people looking for?
Look, listen, and circle the letter in column A.**

	A		B
1. (a.) Rice	b. Bread		Aisle __3__
2. a. Milk	(b.) Cooking Oil		Aisle __5__
3. (a.) carrots	b. oranges		Aisle __2__

Listen again and write the aisle number in column B.

B. Look, listen, and circle the food the people want to buy.

butter　(cake)　(ground beef)　(lettuce)　milk

onions　pepper　(potatoes)　(tomatoes)　eggs

**C. Listen. Look at the food you circled in B.
Check off the groceries they bought.
Then answer the questions.**

1. What did they forget? _____ cake _____

2. What extra item did Francisco buy? _____ candy _____

62　　　　　　　　　　　　　　　　　　　　　　　　　　Unit 5

PREPARATION

If necessary, review food names and the language used for asking for directions. Use pictures and/or realia, and the supermarket map. Have students name food, supermarket sections, and aisle numbers. Provide any reinforcement necessary. See "Reinforcing Vocabulary" on page vi.

PRESENTATION

A and B. Have students read the directions. Make sure they understand that they will hear the dialog several times to complete the two different parts of the activity. Have students complete the activity as you play the tape or read the Listening Transcript aloud several times. Then have them listen again and complete the second part of the activity. Check students' work.

C. Have students listen and complete the activity independently as you play the tape or read the Listening Transcript aloud two or more times. Check students' work.

WORKBOOK

Unit 5, Page 36, Exercise 5.

FOLLOW-UP

Organized Shopping: Have pairs of students talk about times they forgot something on their shopping lists and what they did about it. Have partners tell each other's stories to the class.

♦ Have each student plan a simple menu and make a shopping list of the main ingredients. Then have students organize their shopping lists by supermarket sections.

COMPETENCIES (page 63)
Identify kinds of food
Read price tags and expiration dates

Reading

A. Look and read.

Many food packages have expiration dates.
Before the date, the food is good.
After the date, the food is bad.
Today's date is 9/22/94. Is the food good or bad?
Circle the expiration dates of the good food.

1.

2.

3.

4.

5.

 B. You bought the eggs, the cheese, and the bread. Is the receipt correct? Circle the mistake.

Food Fair Market

Thanks for shopping at
Food Fair !

cheese	$ 2.25
eggs	(.99)
bread	1.89

Unit 5   63

PREPARATION

If necessary, review food names and the numerical representation of the months of the year. Use pictures and/or realia, and food containers that show expiration dates. Review the meaning of **cents** and **dollar,** if necessary.

Teaching Note: You may want to discuss with students the types of food that have expiration dates and how long different kinds of food can be kept safely.

PRESENTATION

A. Have students preview the pictures before they begin. See "Prereading" on page vii. Encourage them to say everything they can about the pictures. Write their ideas on the board or restate them in acceptable English. Have students say which foods are good and which are bad.

B. Have students read and complete the activity independently. Check students' work.

WORKBOOK

Unit 5, Page 36, Exercise 6.

FOLLOW-UP

What's Fresh? Have students bring in pictures of their favorite food. Have students work in small groups. Ask them to describe how these food items are stored and kept fresh. Have students organize food items according to which must be eaten soon and which can be stored for a longer period of time. Ask several groups to report to the class.

♦ Bring in, or have students bring in, food packages and look for expiration dates and any information about the way the food should be stored. Have volunteers display their packages and tell about the information they found.

Identify kinds of food

Write shopping lists

Structure Base

A. Study the examples.

I want	a	potato.
	an	egg.
	some	eggs.
		potatoes.

I want some	lettuce.
	water.

B. Complete the dialog. Use the words from A.

➤ What do we need to make breakfast?

● ___Some___ eggs and ___a___ potato.

➤ We need ___an___ onion and ___some___ bread, too.

● Yes, and ___some___ milk. Oh, and ___some___ butter.

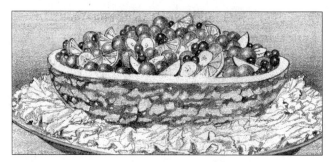

C. Complete the dialog. Write a, an, or some.

➤ Let's make fruit salad.

● OK. I'll write ___a___ shopping list.

➤ Buy ___some___ grapes and ___an___ orange. Buy

___an___ apple and ___a___ banana.

● What about ___a___ watermelon?

➤ Good idea. Buy ___some___ lettuce, too.

64   Unit 5

PREPARATION

If necessary, review the vocabulary in the language boxes with students before they open their books. Use pictures and/or realia. Group pictures or items to review **How much?** and **How many?** Review **a, an,** and **some** using single and multiple items. Remind them that **an** is used before words that begin with **a, e, i, o,** or **u,** or a vowel sound.

PRESENTATION

A. Have students read the language boxes independently. Have students use the words in the language boxes to say as many sentences as they can. Explain to students that they can refer to the language boxes throughout the unit to check or review sen-

tence patterns.

B and **C.** Demonstrate by reading the first sentence aloud and completing the second sentence on the board. Have students complete the activity. Have several students read their answers aloud while the other students check their own answers.

D. Study the examples.

How	much	lettuce	do you want?
		water	
	many	eggs	
		potatoes	

E. Bill's writing Jennifer's shopping list.
Read the answers. Write the questions.

➤ How many potatoes do you want?
● I want **8 potatoes.**

➤ How much cheese do you want?
● I want **a pound of cheese.**

➤ How many bananas do you want?
● I want **7 bananas.**

➤ How much ground beef do you want?
● I want **2 pounds of ground beef.**

 F. Work with a partner.
Use the language in E to talk about food you want.
Write your partner's list.

SHOPPING LIST

PRESENTATION

D. Follow the procedure in A.

E. Demonstrate by reading the first answer aloud and writing the first question on the board. Have students complete the activity. Have several students read the questions aloud to the class.

F. Demonstrate with a student by using the language in E to ask and answer questions about food that you and the student want. Have students complete the activity in pairs. Have several pairs of students present their dialogs to the class.

WORKBOOK

Unit 5, Pages 37–38, Exercises 7A–7B.

FOLLOW-UP

Word Game: Divide the class into groups of three or four. Have each group make a three-column chart labeled **some, a,** and **an** on a sheet of paper or on the board. Hold up pictures of food and have students write the name of each food in the appropriate column. As an example, you might hold up a picture of an apple and show students that **apple** should be written in the **an** column. Have several groups read their lists while the class checks their answers.

♦ Have students make three-column charts labeled **some, a,** and **an** on sheets of paper. Have them see how many food items they can list in each column. Have volunteers read their lists to the class.

COMPETENCIES (page 66)
Identify kinds of food
Write shopping lists

Write It Down

A. Here are meals for one day. Look at the pictures.

Breakfast   Lunch   Dinner

Write a shopping list for the meals in the pictures.

Shopping List

eggs	carrots
butter	lettuce
bread	tomato
cheese	
apple	
milk	
cookies	
chicken	

 B. What do you want for breakfast, lunch, and dinner? Write your shopping list on a sheet of paper.

66   Unit 5

PREPARATION

If necessary, review food names. Explain the usual times of day for breakfast, lunch, and dinner in the U.S.

Culture Note: You might mention that in the U.S. the evening meal is sometimes called supper. The evening meal is often the largest meal of the day. You may also mention that breakfast in the U.S. is often a larger meal than typical breakfasts are in other countries.

PRESENTATION

A. Have students talk about the pictures. Encourage them to say everything they can about them. Write their ideas on the board or restate them in acceptable English. Have

students complete the activity independently. Ask several students to read their complete shopping lists while the rest of the class checks their answers.

About You B. Use the pictures or the supermarket newspaper circulars to help students get ideas. Have students complete the activity independently. Have pairs of students share their lists. Ask several students to read their lists for the class.

WORKBOOK

Unit 5, Page 39, Exercise 8.

FOLLOW-UP

Favorite Meals: Divide the class into small groups. Have group members tell each other about their favorite

meals and the most important ingredients in them. Have each group choose one meal to tell the rest of the class about.

♦ Have students write menus for their favorite meals and shopping lists to go with them. Have volunteers read their menus and lists to the class.

COMPETENCIES
(pages 67 and 68)
Identify kinds of food
Read price tags

One To One   Student A

I. Practice the dialog.

> ➤ How much are **eggs** at **Food World?**
> ● **89 cents.**

2. You want to know the prices at Food World.
Student B has the ad.
Ask Student B. Follow the dialog in I.
Write the prices.

broccoli	59¢
eggs	89¢
milk	$1.79
tomatoes	59¢

3. Student B wants to know the prices at Food Mart.
Use this ad. Follow the dialog in I.

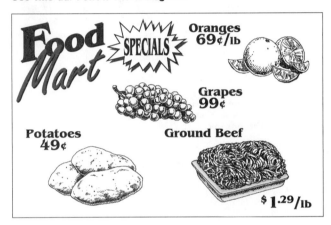

4. Switch roles. Turn to page 68. Complete 2 and 3.

Unit 5   67

PREPARATION

If necessary, review food names, packaging terms, and terms for money. Point out the use of **lb.** as an abbreviation for **pound.**

Teaching Note: You may want to point out the two ways of saying dollars-and-cents amounts. Write **$2.40** on the board. Say, *you can say two dollars and forty cents or two forty.*

PRESENTATION

Teaching Note: For more information on these pages, see "One to One" on page vii.

1. Have students find partners. Assign the roles of A and B. Explain that Student A looks only at page A (page 67) and Student B only at page B (page 68). Have them turn to the appropriate pages. Have students talk about the supermarket ads. Then present the dialog. See "Presenting Dialogs" on page vi.

2. Have students read the directions independently. Model the activity with a student. Then have students complete the activity.

3. Have students read the directions independently and complete the activity.

4. Have students read the directions and complete the activity. You may want students to switch partners at this time, too. Then check students' answers for both pages.

WORKBOOK

Unit 5, Page 40, Exercise 9.

FOLLOW-UP

Bargains: Have students work in pairs. Give each pair a supermarket circular and have them take turns asking about items and their prices. Have several pairs present their conversations to the class.

♦ Have pairs of students compare circulars from two different supermarkets. Have them look for similar items, compare prices, and check for sale items. Have them tell the rest of the class which store they think has the best food bargains.

Identify kinds of food

Read price tags

One To One   Student B

1. Practice the dialog.

> ➤ How much are **eggs** at **Food World**?
> ● 89 cents.

**2. Student A wants to know the prices at Food World.
Use this ad. Follow the dialog in 1.**

**3. You want to know the prices at Food Mart.
Student A has the ad.
Ask Student A. Follow the dialog in 1.
Write the prices.**

grapes	99¢
potatoes	49¢
oranges	69¢
ground beef	$1.29

4. Switch roles. Turn to page 67. Complete 2 and 3.

PRESENTATION

Follow the instructions on page 67.

Extension

COMPETENCIES (page 69)
Identify kinds of food
Identify food packaging

 A. Look at the food. Which do you eat?

B. Look at the food. How is the food packaged? Read the words.

1. box   2. bag   3. jar   4. carton   5. bottle

 C. How is the food in A and B packaged? Write the package.

1. a ___box___ of cereal

2. a ___jar___ of honey

3. a ___bottle___ of soy sauce

4. a ___bag___ of sugar

5. a ___carton___ of milk

Unit 5   69

PREPARATION

Use pictures and/or realia to present or review the new food and the containers. Follow these suggestions.

● Hold up pictures or realia of the food and the container and name each one. Have students repeat. Have students name food items that would be packaged in each type of container.

Culture Note: You may want to discuss recycling with students. You might explain that consumers often recycle glass and plastic bottles, and aluminum cans. You might mention any recycling programs in your community.

PRESENTATION

 A. Have students look at the picture. Encourage them to say everything they can about it. Write their ideas on the board or restate them in acceptable English. You might ask students which food they have never tried and which food they like. Are any of them their favorites? Are there any they don't like?

B. Demonstrate by reading the first word aloud. Have several students read the words aloud.

C. Have students look at the pictures in A and B. Demonstrate by completing the first item on the board. Then write one food from B and its package on the board. Have students complete the

activity independently. Check students' work.

WORKBOOK

Unit 5, Page 40, Exercise 10.

FOLLOW-UP

Packages: Have students work in pairs. Give each pair a supermarket circular and have them talk about the packages that appear on the pages. Have each pair describe the packages in their circular for the class.

♦ Ask small groups of students to devise new packaging for a familiar food. Have them explain the advantages of their new package to the class.

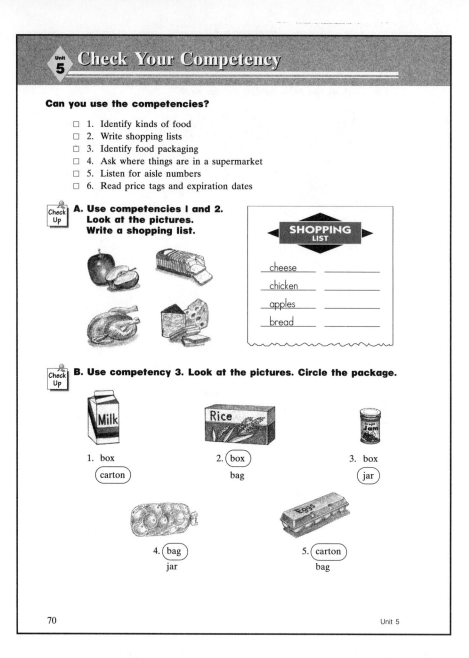

Can you use the competencies?

☐ 1. Identify kinds of food
☐ 2. Write shopping lists
☐ 3. Identify food packaging
☐ 4. Ask where things are in a supermarket
☐ 5. Listen for aisle numbers
☐ 6. Read price tags and expiration dates

Check Up

A. Use competencies 1 and 2.
Look at the pictures.
Write a shopping list.

SHOPPING LIST

cheese _____ _____
chicken _____ _____
apples _____ _____
bread _____ _____

Check Up

B. Use competency 3. Look at the pictures. Circle the package.

1. box
   (carton)

2. (box)
   bag

3. box
   (jar)

4. (bag)
   jar

5. (carton)
   bag

PRESENTATION

Use any of the procedures in "Evaluation," page viii, with these pages. For exercise D, play the tape or read the Listening Transcript to the class two or more times. Record individuals' results on the Unit 5 Individual Competency Chart. Record the class's results on the Class Cumulative Competency Chart.

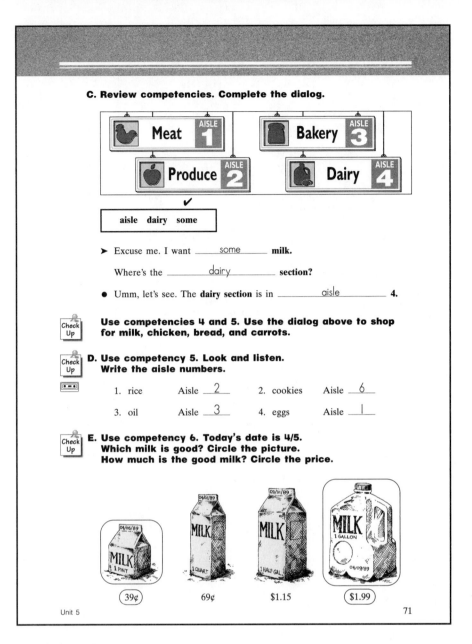

C. Review competencies. Complete the dialog.

| Meat | AISLE 1 | | Bakery | AISLE 3 |
| Produce | AISLE 2 | | Dairy | AISLE 4 |

✔

| aisle dairy some |

➤ Excuse me. I want _____some_____ **milk.**

Where's the _____dairy_____ **section?**

● Umm, let's see. The **dairy section** is in _____aisle_____ **4.**

Check Up **Use competencies 4 and 5. Use the dialog above to shop for milk, chicken, bread, and carrots.**

Check Up **D. Use competency 5. Look and listen. Write the aisle numbers.**

1. rice   Aisle _2_   2. cookies   Aisle _6_

3. oil   Aisle _3_   4. eggs   Aisle _1_

Check Up **E. Use competency 6. Today's date is 4/5. Which milk is good? Circle the picture. How much is the good milk? Circle the price.**

(39¢)   69¢ $1.15   ($1.99)

FOLLOW-UP

ENGLISH IN ACTION

An Optional Cooperative Learning Project: You may want to have students work together to create a class cookbook of their favorite easy-to-fix recipes. Ask each student to contribute one or more recipes. Remind students to list all ingredients and help them write the directions. Suggest that they include a shopping list for each recipe and the names of markets where any unusual ingredients can be purchased.

Students might choose a title and design a cover for the book. Copy the pages and the cover, and have students staple them together to complete the books. Give each stu-dent a copy. Remind students to tell the class about any recipes they try.

Unit 6 Overview

UNIT WARM-UP

The focus of Unit 6, "Shopping," is describing and buying clothing. To stimulate a discussion, you might bring in an article of clothing and pantomime selecting and purchasing it. Encourage students to tell about their experiences and/or difficulties in shopping for clothes for themselves or their families.

Unit 6 Optional Materials

● Picture cards of articles of clothing, color cards, and several size charts from mail-order clothing catalogs. (Mail-order clothing catalogs and department store clothing circulars are good sources for pictures and can be used in activities throughout the unit.)

● An overhead transparency of a blank check.

● A tape measure.

● Clothing price tags and receipts.

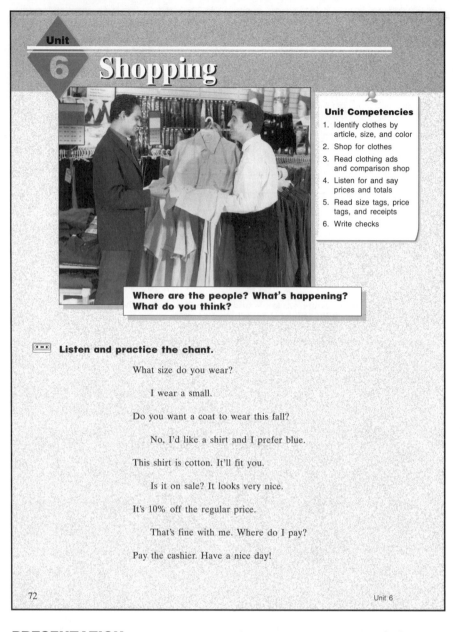

Unit

6 Shopping

Unit Competencies

1. Identify clothes by article, size, and color
2. Shop for clothes
3. Read clothing ads and comparison shop
4. Listen for and say prices and totals
5. Read size tags, price tags, and receipts
6. Write checks

Where are the people? What's happening? What do you think?

Listen and practice the chant.

What size do you wear?

I wear a small.

Do you want a coat to wear this fall?

No, I'd like a shirt and I prefer blue.

This shirt is cotton. It'll fit you.

Is it on sale? It looks very nice.

It's 10% off the regular price.

That's fine with me. Where do I pay?

Pay the cashier. Have a nice day!

72   Unit 6

COMPETENCIES (page 72)

Identify clothes by article, size, and color

Shop for clothes

PREPARATION

Use pantomime and picture cards to preteach the new language in the chant. Follow these suggestions.

● Hold up picture cards and name each item to present **coat** and **shirt.** Have students repeat.

● Discuss **on sale** and how it differs from **for sale.** Define **cashier.**

● You may also want to preteach other expressions in the chant: **What size do you wear? It'll fit you. That's fine with me.**

PRESENTATION

Focus attention on the photo and have students answer the questions. Encourage them to say everything they can about it. Write their ideas on the board or restate them in acceptable English.

Present the chant. See "Presenting Chants" on page vi.

WORKBOOK

Unit 6, Page 41, Exercise 1.

FOLLOW-UP

Pantomime: Bring a coat and a shirt to class. Have pairs of students use them as props to pantomime the chant as the class says it and you read it. Invite other individual stu-

dents to say the chant and have other pairs continue the pantomimes.

◆ Have students work in pairs. Ask them to tell their partners the name and color of an article of clothing they would like to buy. Have students tell the class about their partners' choices.

Starting Out

A. Look and read.

1. Mr. Tran has a job interview.
   He wants a new suit and tie.
   Shirts are on sale.
   He's buying a new shirt, too.

2. It's winter.
   Ms. Barker wants a winter coat.
   Hats and gloves are on sale.
   She's buying a hat, too.
   She doesn't want gloves.

B. Practice the dialog.

➤ I want to buy **a new suit for work.**
● OK. What color do you want?
➤ **Brown or blue.**
● **This blue suit is** nice. I think **it's** your size.
➤ Can I try **it** on?
● Yes, of course. The dressing room is around the corner.
➤ Thank you.

 C. Work with a partner.
Use the dialog in B to shop for clothes you want to buy.

Unit 6   73

PREPARATION

Use the pictures and color cards to preteach the new language. Follow these suggestions.

● To present **suit, tie, hat,** and **gloves,** hold up a picture card for each, say the name, and have students repeat.

● Hold up color cards for **brown** and **blue,** say the names, and have students repeat.

● Clarify **job interview, try it on,** and **dressing room,** and review **on sale,** if necessary.

Teaching Note: You might review ways of saying dollars-and-cents amounts. Write **$10.95** on the board and explain that it may be said *ten dollars and ninety-five cents* or *ten ninety-five.*

PRESENTATION

A. Have students talk about the photographs. Encourage students to say everything they can about them. Write their ideas on the board or restate them in acceptable English. Play the tape or read the captions aloud while students follow along in their books. Then have students read the captions independently.

B. Present the dialog. See "Presenting Dialogs" on page vi.

C. Demonstrate the activity by discussing with a student clothes you want to buy. Have students complete the activity. Have volunteers present their dialogs to the class.

WORKBOOK

Unit 6, Page 41, Exercise 2.

FOLLOW-UP

Clothing Captions: Have students work in pairs. Ask each pair to choose a picture card or a picture from a mail-order catalog or department store circular. Have students create captions like those in A for their pictures. Have volunteers show their pictures and present their captions to the class.

◆ Have students work independently to choose clothing pictures and write simple captions. Have volunteers display their pictures and read their captions.

Identify clothes by article,
  size, and color

Shop for clothes

Listen for and say prices and totals

Talk It Over

A. **Myra is shopping for a new jacket. Practice the dialog.**

➤ Excuse me. Where are the **jackets?**
● They're over here. What size do you wear?
➤ **Medium. That blue jacket** is nice. How much **is it?**
● **$39.95.** Do you want to try **it** on?
➤ Yes, thanks.
  OK, I'll take **it.**
● Fine. How are you paying, cash or check?
➤ **Cash.**

B. **Look at the clothes.**
   What do you want to buy?
   Circle the numbers.

1   2   3   4

$19.95 $40.00 $24.95 $7.99

 C. **Work with a partner.**
   Use the dialog in A to buy the clothes you circled in B.

74   Unit 6

PREPARATION

Use the picture cards you used with page 73 and size charts to preteach the new language.

● Introduce **jacket, pants, boots,** and **shorts** with picture cards. Say the names and have students repeat after you.

✳ ● Display the size charts and talk about the abbreviations for **small, medium, large,** and **extra-large.** You might draw simple T-shirt shapes on the board in the four sizes and label them.

PRESENTATION

A. Have students talk about the photo. Encourage them to say everything they can about it. Write their ideas on the board or restate them in acceptable English. Then present the dialog. See "Presenting Dialogs" on page vi.

B. Demonstrate by looking at the pictures and naming which item you would buy. Have students complete the activity. Have several students name the items they circled.

C. Demonstrate with a student by using the dialog in A to talk about the item you chose in B. Have students complete the activity. Have several pairs present their dialogs to the class.

WORKBOOK

Unit 6, Page 42, Exercise 3.

FOLLOW-UP

Talking About Clothing: Give pairs of students clothing catalogs or department store circulars. Have partners take turns pointing out articles of clothing for the other to name, tell the colors and sizes it comes in, and its price. Have each student choose one item to describe to the rest of the class.

✳ ◆ Give pairs of students catalogs or circulars. Have each pair look at one page of their catalog. Have partners take turns giving information about an article of clothing and figuring out which article is being described.

Word Bank

A. Study the vocabulary.

Clothes	tie	
belt	T-shirt	
blouse	underwear	
coat		
dress	**Size**	
gloves	small (S)	
hat	medium (M)	
jacket	large (L)	
jeans	extra-large (XL)	
pants		
shirt	dressing room	**Colors**
shorts	sales clerk	black
skirt		blue
socks	shoes	brown
suit	boots	gray
sweater	sneakers	green

orange	
pink	
purple	
red	
white	
yellow	

Useful Language
How much (is it)?
Can I try (it) on?
I'll take (it).
Cash or check?
(It's) on sale.

About You

B. Work with a small group.
What are people in your group wearing?
Complete the chart. Use words from A.

Clothes	Color	Size (optional)
	Answers will vary.	

Unit 6   75

PREPARATION

Preteach or review the new vocabulary before students open their books. Use the clothing picture cards and the color cards you used on page 73. Review sizes small, medium, large, and extra-large. Provide any reinforcement necessary. See "Reinforcing Vocabulary" on page vi.

PRESENTATION

A. Have students scan the list. Define, or have other students define, any words individuals do not recognize. Provide any reinforcement necessary. See "Reinforcing Vocabulary" on page vi. Remind students that they can use this list throughout the unit to look up words, to check spelling, and to find key phrases.

About You

B. Put a simple chart like the one in B on the board. Demonstrate by telling students about the clothes you are wearing and writing the information on the chart. Have students complete the activity. Have several students read the information on their charts to the rest of the class.

WORKBOOK

Unit 6, Pages 42–44, Exercises 4A–4D.

FOLLOW-UP

Figure Out Who: Describe the clothing one student is wearing (give items and colors only) and have students figure out whose clothes you are describing. Then have students give similar descriptions (items and colors only) while the rest of the class figures out whose clothes are being described.

♦ Have students write descriptions of their own clothing on 3" x 5" cards, giving items and colors only. Shuffle the cards and pass them out. Have each student read a card and figure out whose clothes are being described.

Identify clothes by article,
   size, and color

Shop for clothes

Read size tags, price tags,
   and receipts

Listen for and say prices
   and totals

Listening

 A. Look, listen, and circle the letter of the correct tag.

1.

2.

3.

1.
a. **L $10.00**
b. **M $10.00**

2.
a. **M $7.99**
b. **M $9.99**

3.
(a.) **XL $24.00**
b. **L $26.00**

 B. What are the people buying?
   Look, listen, and number the pictures in column A.

A	B	C
1 [shoes]	$10.00	cash / (check) / didn't buy
3 [hat]	$15.00	cash / check / (didn't buy)
2 [t-shirt]	$5.00	(cash) / check / didn't buy

 Listen again and write the price in column B.

Listen again. Did the people buy the clothes?
How did they pay?
Circle *cash*, *check*, or *didn't buy* in column C.

Unit 6

PREPARATION

If necessary, use the picture cards,
color cards, and size charts you used
with page 74 to review articles of
clothing, colors, and sizes. Use price
tags and cash register or other
receipts to clarify **prices, tag,** and
receipt. Explain **bargain** and review
dressing room and methods of payment, if necessary. Provide any reinforcement necessary. See
"Reinforcing Vocabulary" on
page vi.

sales clerk
cashier

Teaching Note: The concept of
taxation is presented in Level 2. If
students ask about sales tax, explain that this money goes to the
government.

PRESENTATION

 A. Have students read the
directions. Make sure they
understand that they are to circle a
letter to complete the activity. Have
students complete the activity as you
play the tape or read the Listening
Transcript aloud two or more times.
Check students' work.

B. Have students read the
directions for the first part of
the activity. Make sure they understand that they will number the pictures in column A. Have students
complete the activity as you play the
tape or read the Listening Transcript
aloud two or more times.

Follow the same procedure for the
remaining parts of B. Check students' work.

WORKBOOK

Unit 6, Page 45, Exercise 5.

FOLLOW-UP

Dialogs: Provide pairs with receipts.
Have them create dialogs like those
in A and B. Have volunteers present
their conversations to the class.

◆ Give pairs of students clothing catalogs or circulars. Have students take
turns adding up the prices for two or
three articles they want to buy and
checking each other's addition.
Use play money.

Real-Life English

Reading

A. Look and read.

| Fits sizes 8–11 $5.00 | Medium $15.00 | Medium $15.00 | Size 10 $19.00 |

John's buying these clothes. The clothes are on sale.

1. What's John buying?
2. How much does each item cost?

 B. Read the receipt. Count John's change. Answer the questions.

RECEIPT

socks	$ 5.00
sweater	15.00
sweater	15.00
sneakers	19.00
Subtotal	54.00
Tax	2.70
Total	56.70
Amount Paid	60.00
Change	3.30

1. How much money did John give to the cashier? $60.00

2. How much change did John get? $2.03

3. Did John get the right change?   no

**C. Work with a small group.
What do you think John should do?**

Identify clothes by article, size, and color

Shop for clothes

Read size tags, price tags, and receipts

Listen for and say prices and totals

PREPARATION

If necessary, review articles of clothing and sizes. Follow the procedure on page 74. Use real receipts to present **receipt** and **change**.

PRESENTATION

A. Have students preview the picture and the sales receipt before they read the sentences. See "Prereading" on page vii. Encourage them to say everything they can about them. Write their ideas on the board or restate them in acceptable English. Have students read the sentences independently.

B. Have students look at the receipt and the picture of the bills and coins. Demonstrate by reading the first question aloud and writing the answer on the board. Have students complete the activity independently. Check students' work.

C. Read the directions and the question with students. Then have students talk about their opinions in small groups. Have each group choose one answer to tell the rest of the class.

Culture Note: Tell students that in the U.S. many stores accept returned clothing if it has not been worn; however, it is important to keep receipts as most stores require them for exchanges or refunds.

WORKBOOK

Unit 6, Page 45, Exercise 6.

FOLLOW-UP

Checking Receipts: Create several receipts like the one on the Student Book page. Include errors on some of the receipts. Give pairs of students receipts and have them work together to decide if their receipts are correct or not. Have each pair tell the rest of the class about their receipts.

♦ Give each student a receipt. Have students look for errors, correct them in writing, and show their receipts to the rest of the class.

Identify clothes by article,
size, and color

Shop for clothes

Read size tags, price tags,
and receipts

Structure Base

A. Study the examples.

| I want | this | shirt. |
| | that | |

| I want | these | shoes. |
| | those | |

**B. Lily's daughter, Sonia, wants new clothes for school.
Sonia and Lily are shopping together.
Complete the dialog. Write the correct word.**

➤ Mom, I want _____this_____ **(this, these)** sweater.

● OK, Sonia. I'll buy _____that_____ **(that, those)** sweater for you.

➤ Thanks. I want _____these_____ **(this, these)** shoes and

_____those_____ **(that, those)** socks.

● Well, you have money, too. You can buy

_____those_____ **(that, those)** shoes and socks.

➤ OK.

C. Study the examples.

What size	do	I	wear?
		we	
		you	
		they	
	does	he	
		she	

I	wear	size 8.
We		
You		
They		
He	wears	
She		

78   Unit 6

PREPARATION

If necessary, review the vocabulary
in the language boxes with students
before they open their books.

PRESENTATION

A. Have students read the language
boxes independently. Have students
use the words in the language boxes
to say as many sentences as they can.
Explain to students that they can
refer to the language boxes throughout the unit to check or review sentence patterns.

B. Demonstrate by writing the first
sentence on the board. Have students
complete the activity. Have volunteers read their sentences aloud.

C. Follow the procedure in A.

D. The salesclerk is helping Sonia find a jacket.
   Complete the dialog. Follow the examples in C.

- ■ <u>What</u> color <u>do</u> you want?

- ➤ I want red.

- ■ <u>What</u> size <u>do</u> you wear?

- ➤ I don't know. Mom, <u>what</u> size <u>do</u> I wear?

- ● You <u>wear</u> a large.

E. Study the examples.

Do	I we you they	wear a small?
Does	he she	

Yes,	I she	do. does.

No,	I she	don't. doesn't.

F. Sonia wants gloves, too. Lily is helping Sonia find gloves.
   Complete the dialog. Follow the examples in E.

- ➤ <u>Do</u> you <u>like</u> green?

- ● No, I <u>don't</u>.

- ➤ <u>Do</u> you <u>like</u> black?

- ➤ Yes, I <u>do</u>.

 G. Work with a partner.
   You and your partner are shopping for clothes together.
   Follow the examples in A, C, and E to talk about
   clothes you want.

PRESENTATION

D. Follow the procedure in B.

E. Follow the procedure in A.

F. Follow the procedure in B.

G. Use the language patterns in A, C, and E to tell a student about clothes you want. Have students complete the activity. Have several pairs of students present their dialogs to the class.

WORKBOOK

Unit 6, Pages 45–46, Exercises 7A–7C.

FOLLOW-UP

✳ **Shopping for Clothes:** Have students *Use real clothes* work in groups of three. Give each group a clothing catalog or department store circular. Have them use the clothing pictured to create conversations about shopping for clothing. Suggest that two students play the shoppers and one student, the clerk. Have groups present their conversations to the class.

♦ Have pairs of students use catalogs and circulars to write short question-and-answer dialogs like those in D and F. Have volunteers read their dialogs to the class.

Write It Down

A. Look at the check. Answer the questions.

```
Luisa Gamboa                                          680
601 Madison Ave.
Albany, NY 12212
                                    June 3   19 94

PAY TO THE    Buy-Mart                          $  26.59
ORDER OF
Twenty-six and  59/100                              DOLLARS

TOWN BANK
700 Hamiton St.
Albany, NY 12204
FOR _____        Luisa Gamboa

ı"ııı9046031:6055000ı
```

1. How much is the check for? _____ $26.59 _____
2. Who's writing the check? _____ Luisa Gamboa _____
3. Who's receiving the check? _____ Buy-Mart _____
4. What's the date of the check? _____ June 3, 1994 _____

About You
B. Write a check for $49.95 to Smart Mart.
   Print your name and address.
   Write today's date. Sign your name.

```
_____ Answers will vary. _____            164

_____      19 _____

PAY TO THE    Smart Mart                        $  49.95
ORDER OF
Forty-nine and  95/100                              DOLLARS

LANDMARK BANK
125 Shady Lane
Shamrock, Texas 79079
FOR _____

ı"ııı9046031:6055000ı
```

PREPARATION

To introduce check writing, use an overhead transparency of a blank check. Identify the parts of a check and demonstrate how to write one.

Teaching Note: You may want to remind students to proofread the information they write on checks to make sure it is correct. Also, remind them that money orders can be used in place of checks, and that they should always keep their money order receipts.

PRESENTATION

A. Have students look at the check. Encourage them to say everything they can about it. Write their ideas on the board or restate them in acceptable English. Have students complete the activity independently. Ask several students to read their answers aloud while the rest of the class checks their answers.

About You **B.** Use the overhead transparency and the list to review parts of the check, if necessary. Have students complete the activity independently. Check students' work.

WORKBOOK

Unit 6, Page 47, Exercise 8.

FOLLOW-UP

Writing Checks: Draw a blank check for a fictitious bank and make several copies. In two columns on the board, write names of several payees and several dollars-and-cents amounts. Give each pair of students several checks and have them choose from the names and amounts on the board to practice writing checks.

♦ Have small groups of students brainstorm situations in which they might write checks. Provide drawings of blank checks to each group and have them write checks for the situations. Have each group present one situation and check to the rest of the class.

One To One   Student A

I. Two friends want some new clothes.
Clothes are on sale at Buy-Mart and at Smart Shop.
One friend has the Smart Shop ad.
The other has the Buy-Mart ad.
Practice the dialog.

➤ Are **jackets** on sale at **Smart Shop?**
● Yes, they are.
➤ How much are they?
● They're $40.00.

 2. Find out the prices at Smart Shop. Ask Student B.
Follow the dialog in I. Write the information.

a. ___$40.00___   b. ___$10.00___   c. ___$18.00___

 3. Tell Student B the prices at Buy-Mart.
Follow the dialog in I.

4. Switch roles. Turn to page 82. Complete 2 and 3.

COMPETENCIES
(pages 81 and 82)

Identify clothes by article, size, and color

Read clothing ads and comparison shop

PREPARATION

If necessary, review names for articles of clothing and ways to say dollars-and-cents amounts. Follow the instructions in "Preparation" on page 74.

PRESENTATION

Teaching Note: For more information on these pages, see "One to One" on page vii.

1. Have students find partners. Assign the roles of A and B. Explain that Student A looks only at page A (page 81) and Student B only at page B (page 82). Have them turn to the appropriate pages. Have students talk about the ads. Then present the dialog. See "Presenting Dialogs" on page vi.

2. Have students read the directions independently. Model the activity with a student. Then have students complete the activity.

3. Have students read the directions independently and complete the activity.

4. Have students read the directions and complete the activity. You may want students to switch partners at this time, too. Check students' answers for both pages.

WORKBOOK

Unit 6, Page 47, Exercise 9.

FOLLOW-UP

Store Ads: Bring in clothing sale ads from local stores. Have students work in small groups to look for the best bargains. Have each group choose one member to tell the rest of the class about the group's best buys.

♦ Have pairs of students design store ads featuring sale items like the ads on these pages. Have each pair show their ad to the rest of the class.

Identify clothes by article,
size, and color

Read clothing ads and
comparison shop

One To One   Student B

1. **Two friends want some new clothes.**
   Clothes are on sale at Buy-Mart and at Smart Shop.
   One friend has the Smart Shop ad.
   The other has the Buy Mart ad.
   Practice the dialog.

   ➤ Are **jackets** on sale at **Smart Shop?**
   ● Yes, they are.
   ➤ How much are they?
   ● They're **$40.00.**

2. **Tell Student A the prices at Smart Shop.**
   Follow the dialog in I.

3. **Find out the prices at Buy-Mart. Ask Student A.**
   Follow the dialog in I. Write the information.

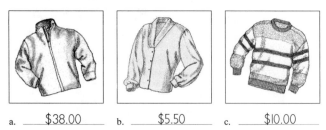

   a. ___$38.00___   b. ___$5.50___   c. ___$10.00___

4. **Switch roles. Turn to page 8I. Complete 2 and 3.**

PRESENTATION

Follow the instructions on page 81.

COMPETENCIES (page 83)
Identify clothes by article,
size, and color

Extension

A. Look at the charts. Which chart has your sizes?

WOMEN'S SIZES									
Size	P	S		M		L		XL	
	4	6	8	10	12	14	16	18	20
Chest	33	34	35	36	38	40	42	44	46
Waist	25	26	27	28	29	31	32	34	35
Hips	35	36	38	39	40	42	43	45	46

MEN'S SIZES				
Size	S	M	L	XL
Neck	14–14 ½	15–15 ½	16–16 ½	17–17 ½
Chest	34–36	38–40	42–44	46–48
Waist	28–30	32–34	36–38	40–42
Sleeve	32–33	33–34	34–35	35–36

B. Use the chart in A that has your sizes. Write your sizes.

Women

	Number Size	Letter Size
Dress	_____	_____
Blouse	_____	_____
Skirt	_____ (waist)	_____
Pants and jeans	_____ (hips)	_____

Men

	Number Size	Letter Size
Shirt	_____ (neck)	_____
	_____ (sleeve)	
Pants and jeans	_____ (waist)	
Suit coat and sport coat	_____ (chest)	_____
	_____ (sleeve)	

Unit 6   83

PREPARATION

Use pictures and/or realia to present or review the new language. Follow these suggestions.

● Use the tape measure to show students the correlation between body measurements in inches and number and letter sizes.

● Use the mail-order catalog size charts to introduce or review **sleeve, neck, chest, waist,** and **hips.**

Teaching Note: Explain that students do not have to talk about their sizes if they do not want to. They can talk about someone else's size, or make one up instead.

PRESENTATION

A. Have students look at the charts.

Encourage them to say everything they can about them. Write their ideas on the board or restate them in acceptable English. Then have them answer the question.

B. Demonstrate by making a simple chart like the one on the page on the board and filling in your sizes or fictitious sizes. Remind students they do not need to use their own sizes. Have students complete the activity. Check students' work.

WORKBOOK

Unit 6, Page 48, Exercise 10.

FOLLOW-UP

Family Shopping: Provide students with several size charts, including some that show children's sizes. Have them work in small groups to talk about what sizes all the members of their families wear.

♦ Have students work independently. Have them use size charts to put together size lists for each member of their families. Suggest that they use these as a handy reference when they go shopping for clothes.

Can you use the competencies?

☐ 1. Identify clothes by article, size, and color
☐ 2. Shop for clothes
☐ 3. Read clothing ads and comparison shop
☐ 4. Listen for and say prices and totals
☐ 5. Read size tags, price tags, and receipts
☐ 6. Write checks

A. Review competencies 1 and 2. Complete the dialog.

| color   much   size   take |

➤ I want **a new winter coat.**

● What _____size_____ do you wear?

➤ **Medium.**

● What _____color_____ do you want?

➤ I want **blue.** How _____much_____ is that blue coat?

● It's **$39.00.**

➤ OK, I'll _____take_____ it.

 **Use competencies 1 and 2.
Use the dialog above to talk about
clothes you want to buy.**

 **B. Use competency 3. Look at the ads. Where would
you shop? Circle the number of the ad. Tell why.**

1.

Long's Department Store   SALE
$30.00 $40.00 $13.00

②.

W ARE'S DEPARTMENT STORE
$24.00 $30.00 $10.00
BIG SAVINGS!

PRESENTATION

Use any of the procedures in "Evaluation," page viii, with these pages. For exercise C, play the tape or read the Listening Transcript to the class two or more times. Record individuals' results on the Unit 6 Individual Competency Chart. Record the class's results on the Class Cumulative Competency Chart.

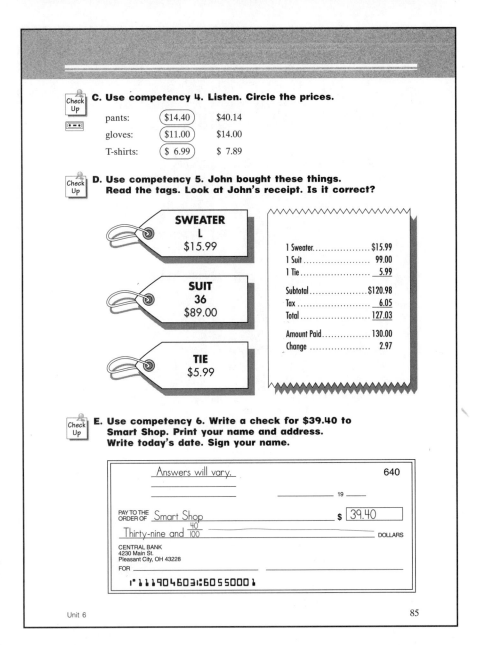

C. Use competency 4. Listen. Circle the prices.

pants:	($14.40)	$40.14
gloves:	($11.00)	$14.00
T-shirts:	($ 6.99)	$ 7.89

D. Use competency 5. John bought these things.
Read the tags. Look at John's receipt. Is it correct?

SWEATER
L
$15.99

SUIT
36
$89.00

TIE
$5.99

1 Sweater.................$15.99
1 Suit 99.00
1 Tie 5.99

Subtotal...................$120.98
Tax 6.05
Total 127.03

Amount Paid............... 130.00
Change 2.97

E. Use competency 6. Write a check for $39.40 to
Smart Shop. Print your name and address.
Write today's date. Sign your name.

Answers will vary.   640

_____   _____ 19 ____

PAY TO THE
ORDER OF Smart Shop $ 39.40

Thirty-nine and 40/100 _____ DOLLARS

CENTRAL BANK
4230 Main St.
Pleasant City, OH 43228
FOR _____   _____

⑈11190460⑆605 5000⑈

Unit 6   85

FOLLOW-UP

ENGLISH IN ACTION

An Optional Cooperative Learning Project: You may want to help students set up a simple store in the classroom and role-play clothes shopping. For merchandise, use picture cards and pictures from catalogs and circulars spread out on desks and/or tables rather than articles of clothing. Help them decide what departments the store should have and group pictures accordingly. Some students can be customers and others, store clerks.

Students might draw and make copies of simple forms for checks and receipts and use play money to make transactions. Have them attach price tags to each item and suggest that they put sale prices on some items.

Set aside some time after the role-play for students to discuss what they learned in setting up the store and taking the roles of customers and clerks.

Unit 7 Overview

UNIT WARM-UP

The focus of Unit 7, "Home," is finding housing, arranging for utilities, and asking for simple household repairs. You might show students pictures of several different kinds of housing (single-family homes, duplexes, high-rise and garden apartments) and talk about the kind of home you live in. Invite students to discuss their experiences in locating housing and making their homes comfortable for themselves and their families.

Unit 7 Optional Materials

● Pictures of a variety of apartments and houses.

● Pictures of a living room, a bedroom, a bathroom, and a kitchen.

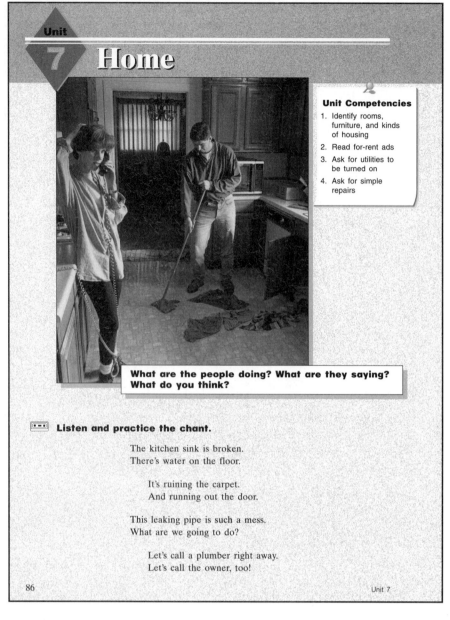

Unit
7

Home

Unit Competencies

1. Identify rooms, furniture, and kinds of housing
2. Read for-rent ads
3. Ask for utilities to be turned on
4. Ask for simple repairs

What are the people doing? What are they saying? What do you think?

Listen and practice the chant.

The kitchen sink is broken.
There's water on the floor.

It's ruining the carpet.
And running out the door.

This leaking pipe is such a mess.
What are we going to do?

Let's call a plumber right away.
Let's call the owner, too!

86

Unit 7

COMPETENCIES (page 86)

Identify rooms, furniture, and kinds of housing
Ask for simple repairs

PREPARATION

Use the pictures of rooms to preteach the new language in the chant. Follow these suggestions.

● Hold up the picture of the kitchen and point out the sink. Have students repeat **kitchen** and **sink** after you. Hold up the picture of the living room and point out the carpet. Have students repeat carpet after you.

● You may also want to preteach other expressions in the chant: **such a mess, right away.**

PRESENTATION

Focus attention on the photo and have students answer the questions. Encourage them to say everything they can about it. Write their ideas on the board or restate them in acceptable English.

Present the chant. See "Presenting Chants" on page vi.

WORKBOOK

Unit 7, Page 49, Exercise 1.

FOLLOW-UP

Pantomime: Have pairs of students pantomime the chant as the class says it. Invite individual students to say the chant and have students continue the pantomimes until everyone who wants to participate has done so.

♦ Have students work in pairs to tell each other about household emergencies they have experienced and what they did. Have students tell each other's stories to the rest of the class.

Starting Out

A. This is Wen-tao and Ji-ling's apartment. Look and read.

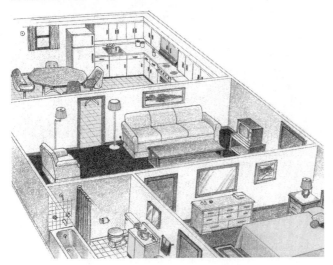

1. Wen-tao likes to cook.
   There's a stove and a refrigerator in the kitchen.
   There's a smoke detector, too.

2. The bedroom's large.
   There's a bed and a dresser in the bedroom.
   There's a rug near the bed.

3. The bathroom's small.
   There's soap on the sink.
   There are towels beside the sink.

4. Wen-tao and Ji-ling visit with friends in the living room.
   They have a nice sofa and chair in the living room.

Wen-tao and Ji-ling like their home.
The rent is $450 a month. The deposit is $200.

B. Answer the questions.

1. What's Wen-tao and Ji-ling's apartment like?
2. How much is the rent? Is that a lot of money?
3. What's your home like?

Unit 7   87

PREPARATION

Use pictures of rooms to preteach the new language.

● To present names of rooms, hold up a picture of each room, name it, and have students repeat.

● Use the pictures of the rooms to present **stove, refrigerator, bed, dresser, sink, sofa,** and **TV.** Have students say each word after you.

Pronunciation Note: If students have difficulty saying **refrigerator,** they can say **fridge** instead.

● Write **rent** and **deposit** on the board and say that rent is paid at regular intervals, usually once a month, while a deposit is paid once, when renters move in. The renters get the deposit back when they move

if they leave the apartment in good condition.

PRESENTATION

A. Have students talk about the picture. Encourage them to say everything they can about it. Write their ideas on the board or restate them in acceptable English. Play the tape or read the sentences aloud while students follow along in their books. Then have students read the sentences independently.

B. Have students answer the questions orally or in writing.

WORKBOOK

Unit 7, Page 49, Exercise 2.

FOLLOW-UP

Home: Have students work in pairs to tell each other what they like about their homes. Have volunteers tell the whole class.

◆ Have students write two or three sentences about what they like about their homes. Have volunteers read their sentences to the class.

COMPETENCIES (page 88)

Identify rooms, furniture, and kinds of housing

kitchen	bedroom	bathroom
bedroom	kitchen	living room
living room	bathroom	kitchen

Sample Bingo Card

Talk It Over

A. Lisa and Cynthia are in the cafeteria. They're talking about their homes. Practice the dialog.

➤ I live in **a house.** What kind of home do you have?
● **An apartment.**
➤ What's it like?
● **Well, there's one bedroom and one bathroom.**
➤ Is the **bedroom large?**
● **Not really.** There's **only a bed, a dresser, and a lamp.**
  I want to **buy some new curtains for the window.**
➤ Oh. I want to **put a new sofa and a coffee table in my living room.**

 B. Write about your home.

Room	What's in the room?
Living Room	Answers will vary.
Kitchen	
Bedroom	
Bathroom	

 C. Work with a partner.
Use the dialog in A to talk about your home.

Unit 7

PREPARATION

Use the pictures of rooms and of houses and apartments to preteach the new language. Follow these suggestions.

● Use the pictures of rooms to preteach or review the names of rooms and furnishings.

● To introduce **house** and **apartment,** hold up the pictures and name each one. Have students repeat.

PRESENTATION

A. Have students talk about the photo. Encourage them to say everything they can about it. Write their ideas on the board or restate them in acceptable English. Then present the dialog. See "Presenting Dialogs" on page vi.

B. Demonstrate by drawing a chart like the one in B on the board and completing it with information about your home. Have students complete the activity.

C. Demonstrate with a student by using the dialog in A to talk about your home. Have students complete the activity. Have several pairs present their dialogs to the class.

WORKBOOK

Unit 7, Page 50, Exercise 3.

FOLLOW-UP

Rooms and Furnishings Bingo: Have students make nine-square bingo grids. Have them write **kitchen, bathroom, bedroom,** and **living room** in any squares they like, putting one room name in each square. Say the name of a piece of furniture that would be found in one of the rooms. Have students write the name of the item in the appropriate square. Remind students that they should put each item in only one square even though it may be found in more than one room. The student who gets the first bingo wins.

♦ Have students help you write a list of furniture on the board. Have students act as bingo callers, picking words from the list at random.

Word Bank

A. Study the vocabulary.

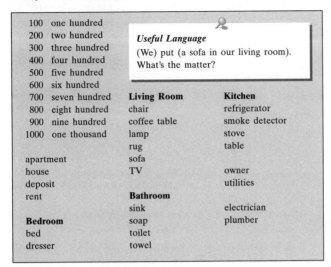

100	one hundred
200	two hundred
300	three hundred
400	four hundred
500	five hundred
600	six hundred
700	seven hundred
800	eight hundred
900	nine hundred
1000	one thousand

Useful Language
(We) put (a sofa in our living room).
What's the matter?

apartment
house
deposit
rent

Bedroom
bed
dresser

Living Room
chair
coffee table
lamp
rug
sofa
TV

Bathroom
sink
soap
toilet
towel

Kitchen
refrigerator
smoke detector
stove
table

owner
utilities

electrician
plumber

 B. Work with a partner. Use words from A to describe the furniture in the living room.

Unit 7

89

PREPARATION

Preteach or review the new vocabulary before students open their books. Give special attention to the numbers. Use the pictures you used with page 87. Provide any reinforcement necessary. See "Reinforcing Vocabulary" on page vi.

PRESENTATION

A. Have students scan the list. Define, or have students define, any words individuals do not recognize. Provide any reinforcement necessary. See "Reinforcing Vocabulary" on page vi. Remind students that they can use this list throughout the unit to look up words, to check spelling, and to find key phrases.

B. Demonstrate by describing one or two items in the picture. Have students work in pairs to complete the activity. Have several students present their descriptions to the class.

Teaching Note: You might use the room pictures to point out where smoke detectors are usually installed. Explain that usually landlords are responsible for installing smoke detectors. You might also mention that it is important to check smoke detector batteries regularly.

WORKBOOK

Unit 7, Pages 50–51, Exercises 4A–4C.

FOLLOW-UP

Descriptions: Have students work in pairs to describe the furniture in another room in their homes. Have several students present their descriptions to the class.

♦ Have students write two- or three-sentence descriptions of the furniture in one room of their homes. Have volunteers read their descriptions to the class.

Transcript p. 148

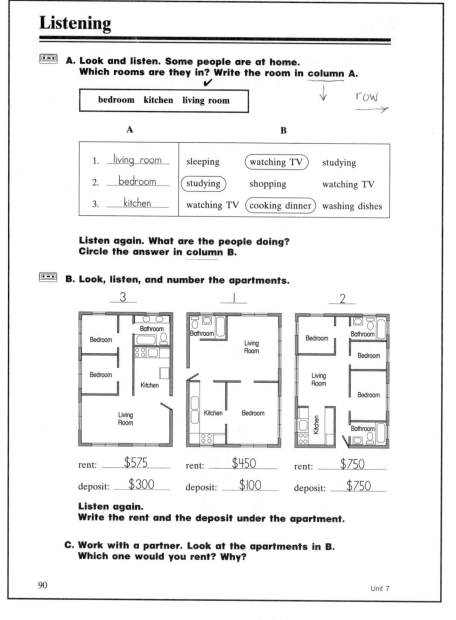

Listening

A. Look and listen. Some people are at home. Which rooms are they in? Write the room in column A.

bedroom   kitchen   living room

↓ row →

	A		B	
1.	living room	sleeping	(watching TV)	studying
2.	bedroom	(studying)	shopping	watching TV
3.	kitchen	watching TV	(cooking dinner)	washing dishes

**Listen again. What are the people doing?
Circle the answer in column B.**

B. Look, listen, and number the apartments.

3   1   2

rent: _$575_   rent: _$450_   rent: _$750_

deposit: _$300_   deposit: _$100_   deposit: _$750_

**Listen again.
Write the rent and the deposit under the apartment.**

**C. Work with a partner. Look at the apartments in B.
Which one would you rent? Why?**

90   Unit 7

PREPARATION

If necessary, review the names of rooms and furniture. Use the pictures you used with page 87.

PRESENTATION

A. Have students read the directions for the first part of the activity. Make sure they understand that they will write their answers in column A. Have students complete the first part of the activity as you play the tape or read the Listening Transcript aloud two or more times.

Have students read the directions for the second part of A. Make sure they understand that they will circle the phrases in column B. Have students complete the activity as you play the

tape or read the Listening Transcript aloud two or more times. Check students' work.

B. Have students read the directions for the first part of the activity. Make sure they understand what they are to do. Have students complete the first part of the activity as you play the tape or read the Listening Transcript aloud two or more times. Follow the same procedure for the second part of B. Check students' work.

C. Demonstrate by saying which apartment you would rent and why. Have students complete the activity. Have several students share their answers with the class.

WORKBOOK

Unit 7, Page 52, Exercise 5.

FOLLOW-UP

Important Information: Have students share ideas on what they think are important things to know before renting an apartment. Take notes on the board.

♦ Have pairs use the notes on the board to create conversations about renting apartments. They might be prospective tenant and landlord or two friends talking over an apartment one has looked at. Have volunteers present their conversations to the class.

Reading

**A. Newspapers have ads with apartments
and houses for rent. Look and read.**

Apts for Rent	Lg 1 bdrm apt.	Apts for Rent	3 bdrm, 2 ba. Lg lv rm, kit.
Furn	Parking. No pets.	**Unfurn**	Near schools and park.
Sm furn 2 bdrm apt.	$350 mo. $200 deposit.	1 bdrm apt, 200 Main St.	$800 mo/$800 deposit.
412 Albany St.	Some utils.	Very nice area.	Utils incl.
$500 mo, $250 deposit.	Bay Apts, 555-9250	$300 rent, $100 deposit.	Call 555-7391
Call 555-0211 after 5.		Sm pet OK. 555-5922	

**B. Read the words. Write the abbreviations.
Use the ads in A.**

1. apartment	_apt_	2. bathroom	_ba_
3. bedroom	_bdrm_	4. furnished	_furn_
5. included	_incl_	6. kitchen	_kit_
7. large	_lg_	8. living room	_lv rm_
9. month	_mo_	10. small	_sm_
11. unfurnished	_unfurn_	12. utilities	_utils_

C. Answer the questions about the ads.

1. Is the apartment on Albany Street furnished?   _yes_

   How many bedrooms are there?   _2_

2. Can you have pets at Bay Apartments?   _no_

   Is there parking?   _yes_

3. How much is the rent for the apartment on
   Main Street?   _$300_

   How much is the deposit?   _$100_

4. How many bathrooms are there in the 3-bedroom
   apartment?   _2_

   Are utilities included?   _yes_

Unit 7   91

PREPARATION

If necessary, review the names for
rooms and the meanings of **rent** and
deposit. Follow the instructions in
"Preparation" on page 87. Use the
pictures of rooms to introduce the
word **utilities** by pointing out the
uses of electricity (electrical appliances, lights), gas (hot water, heat),
and water.

PRESENTATION

A. Have students preview the ads
for a few minutes before they read
them. See "Prereading" on page vii.
Encourage them to say everything
they can about the ads. Write their
ideas on the board or restate them in
acceptable English. Have students
read the ads independently.

B. Demonstrate by writing the
first item on the board. Have
students complete the activity independently. Have several students
read their answers aloud while the
rest of the students check their own
answers.

C. Demonstrate by reading the
first question aloud and writing
the answer on the board. Have students complete the activity independently. Have several students read
their answers aloud while the rest of
the students check their own
answers.

WORKBOOK

Unit 7, Page 52, Exercise 6.

FOLLOW-UP

For-Rent Ads: Have students use
index cards to write ads for their own
homes using abbreviations from the
unit. Shuffle the cards and pass them
out. Have students read the information on their cards aloud to the class,
explaining the abbreviations.

♦ Have students pick new cards and
rewrite the information in the ads
using complete sentences. Post the
ads and descriptions about the room
for the class to read.

Identify rooms, furniture, and
    kinds of housing

Structure Base

A. Study the examples.

| How many | bedrooms | are there? |
| | bathrooms | |

| There | are | two bedrooms. |
| There's | | one bathroom. |

**B. Chris is asking Ms. Orozco about an apartment.
Use the words from A.**

➤ How many bedrooms _____are there_____ ?

● There are _____ **two bedrooms.**

➤ How many bathrooms _____are there_____ ?

● There's _____ **one bathroom.**

C. Study the examples.

| Is | there | a deposit? |
| Are | | rugs in the living room? |

| Yes, there | is. |
| | are. |

| No, there | isn't. |
| | aren't. |

**D. Chris wants to know more about the apartment.
Complete the dialog. Use the words from A and C.**

➤ Are there _____ **rugs in the apartment?**

● There are _____ **rugs in the bedrooms.**

➤ Are there _____ **rugs in the living room?**

● **No,** _____there aren't_____ .

➤ **The ad says the rent is $450.** _____Is there_____ **a deposit?**

● **Yes,** _____there is_____ **. There's a $450 deposit, too.**

92   Unit 7

PREPARATION

If necessary, review the vocabulary
in the language boxes with students
before they open their books. Follow
the instructions in "Preparation" on
page 87.

PRESENTATION

A. Have students read the language
boxes independently. Have students
use the words in the language boxes
to say as many sentences as they can.
Explain to students that they can
refer to the language boxes throughout the unit to check or review sentence patterns.

B. Demonstrate by writing the first
sentence on the board. Have students complete the activity. Have
students read their answers aloud

while the rest of the students check
their own answers.

C. Follow the procedure in A.

D. Follow the procedure in B.

E. Work with a partner. You have an apartment for rent.
Your partner is asking about it.
Follow the dialogs in B and D.

F. Study the examples.

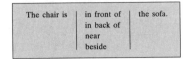

The chair is	in front of	the sofa.
	in back of	
	near	
	beside	

G. Look at the room.
Read the sentences. Write *yes* or *no*.

_____no_____	1.	The coffee table is in back of the chair.
_____yes_____	2.	The coffee table is in front of the sofa.
_____no_____	3.	The lamp is near the TV.
_____yes_____	4.	The lamp is beside the sofa.
_____yes_____	5.	The chair is near the sofa.

 H. Work with a partner. Talk about a room in your home.
Where's the furniture? Follow the examples in F and G.

Unit 7   93

Add furn. to floor plans.

PRESENTATION

E. Demonstrate by saying you have an apartment for rent. Have a student ask you questions about it using the sentence patterns in B and D. Then have students complete the activity. Ask several pairs of students to present their dialogs to the class.

F. Follow the procedure in A.

Teaching Note: You may want to review prepositions of location by standing in back of, in front of, near, and beside your desk. As you stand in each place, say, I'm standing near (beside) my desk.

G. Demonstrate by reading the first sentence and writing the answer on the board. Have students complete the activity. Have students read the sentences and their answers aloud as the rest of the students check their own answers.

H. Demonstrate by telling about the placement of furniture in a room in your home, using the phrases in F. Have students complete the activity in pairs. Have pairs of students present their dialogs to the class.

WORKBOOK

Unit 7, Pages 53–54, Exercises 7A–7C.

FOLLOW-UP

Furniture Arrangements: Show students the floor plans you used with page 90. Ask them to draw simple floor plans that show the arrangement of the furniture in one of the rooms of their homes. Then have them work in pairs and tell each other about the furniture in their floor plans using the phrases in F. Have volunteers show their floor plans to the class and talk about them.

♦ Have students use their floor plans to write two or three sentences about the arrangement of the furniture in one of the rooms of their homes. Have volunteers show their floor plans and read their sentences to the class.

Ask for simple repairs

Write It Down

A. Look and read. What's the matter?

The roof leaks.

The light is broken.

The toilet is
stopped up.

**B. Ms. Anaya wants repairs.
She's writing a note to the owner. Complete the note.** ✔

apartment call plumber stopped toilet

> Dear Mr. Soto,
>   The ___toilet___ in my ___apartment___
> is ___stopped___ up.
>   Please ___call___ a ___plumber___
> right away.
>   Thank you.
>   Ms. Anaya

About You

**C. What's the matter at your house or apartment?
Write a note on a sheet of paper. Ask for repairs.**

94   Unit 7

PREPARATION

Use the pictures of rooms you used with page 86 to talk about the jobs of an electrician and a plumber.

PRESENTATION

Teaching Note: You may want to tell students it is important that they notify their landlords of problems before calling for repairs or trying to fix problems themselves.

A. Have students look at the pictures. Encourage them to say everything they can about them. Write their ideas on the board or restate them in acceptable English. Have students read the captions independently.

B. Have students read the directions. Make sure they understand that they will use words from the box to complete the sentences. Have students complete the activity independently. Have several students read their completed notes aloud while the other students check their own answers.

About You

C. Have students brainstorm other repair problems that can occur in homes. Write them on the board (cracked window, leaky faucet, etc.). Have each student choose one problem and write a note requesting repairs. Have volunteers read their notes to the class.

WORKBOOK

Unit 7, Page 55, Exercise 8.

FOLLOW-UP

Call for Repairs: Have students work in small groups to discuss times when they had to request or arrange for home repairs. Have them tell how the problem was solved. Have each group choose one story to tell the rest of the class.

♦ Have students write two or three sentences about times they had to request or arrange for repairs. Remind them to tell how the problem was solved. Have volunteers read their sentences to the class.

One To One

Student A

I. Practice the dialog.

> ➤ How much is the **rent** at **102 First Street?**
> ● It's **$500.**
> ➤ How many **bedrooms** are there?
> ● **Two.**
> ➤ How many **bathrooms** are there?
> ● **One.**
> ➤ Is it **furnished?**
> ● **No.**

 2. You're calling about the apartments. Ask Student B. Follow the dialog in I. Write the information.

Address:	102 First Street	215 West Avenue
Rent:	$500	$425
Number of bedrooms:	2	1
Number of bathrooms:	1	1
Furnished?	no	yes

3. Student B is calling about the apartments. Tell Student B the information. Follow the dialog in I.

APARTMENTS
1 bdrm, 1 ba furn apt for rent.
210 Oak Avenue
$450 mo., $450 deposit.
Phone 555-3101.

1786 Burgess Street
2 bdrm, 1 ba apt., unfurn.
2nd floor.
$450 rent, $300 deposit.
555-2509.

4. Switch roles. Turn to page 96. Complete 2 and 3.

Identify rooms, furniture, and
kinds of housing

Read for-rent ads

PREPARATION

If necessary, review the names of
rooms and the meanings of **rent** and
deposit. Follow the instructions in
"Preparation" on page 87.

PRESENTATION

Teaching Note: For more information on these pages, see "One to
One" on page vii.

1. Have students find partners.
Assign the roles of A and B. Explain
that Student A looks only at page A
(page 95) and Student B only at page
B (page 96). Have them turn to the
appropriate pages. Have students
talk about the ads. Then present the
dialog. See "Presenting Dialogs" on
page vi.

2. Have students read the
directions independently.
Model the activity with a student.
Then have students complete the
activity.

3. Have students read the directions
independently and complete the
activity.

4. Have students read the directions
and complete the activity. You may
want students to switch partners at
this time, too. Check students'
answers for both pages.

WORKBOOK

Unit 7, Page 56, Exercise 9.

FOLLOW-UP

Finding Housing: Have students
work in pairs. Give each pair a newspaper rental ad section. Have them
discuss what kinds of housing they
would like and help each other look
for housing that meets their criteria.
Have several pairs tell the class what
they found.

♦ Have students write ads describing
their "dream houses." Have volunteers read their ads to the class.

Identify rooms, furniture, and
kinds of housing

Read for-rent ads

One To One   Student B

I. Practice the dialog.

➤ How much is the **rent** at **102 First Street?**
● It's **$500.**
➤ How many **bedrooms** are there?
● **Two.**
➤ How many **bathrooms** are there?
● **One.**
➤ Is it **furnished?**
● **No.**

2. Student A is calling about the apartments.
Tell Student A the information. Follow the dialog in I.

3. You're calling about the apartments. Ask Student A.
Follow the dialog in I. Write the information.

Address:	210 Oak Avenue	1786 Burgess Street
Rent:	$450	$450
Number of bedrooms:	1	2
Number of bathrooms:	1	1
Furnished?	yes	no

4. Switch roles. Turn to page 95. Complete 2 and 3.

96   Unit 7

PRESENTATION

Follow the instructions on page 95.

Extension

 A. Practice the dialog.

> ➤ Hello. **City Gas and Electric.**
> ● I need the **electricity and the gas** turned on at my new **apartment.**
> ➤ What's your address?
> ● **545 Central Street, apartment 28.**
> ➤ And your name?
> ● **Eva Delgado.**
> ➤ OK. We can turn them on **tomorrow afternoon.**
> ● OK. Thank you.

About You **B. Work with a partner.**
You need the water turned on.
Use the dialog in A to call the City Water Company.

*Use cable service
telephone*

Unit 7   97

PREPARATION

Preteach or review the new vocabulary. Follow these suggestions.

● If necessary, review **deposit** and **utilities.** Follow the instructions in "Preparation" on page 91. Tell students that deposits are often required by utilities when service is started and are usually refunded at the end of the service.

PRESENTATION

A. Have students look at the picture. Encourage them to say everything they can about it. Write their ideas on the board or restate them in acceptable English. Then present the dialog. See "Presenting Dialogs" on ✳ page vi.

About You **B.** Demonstrate the activity with a student. Have students complete the activity in pairs. Ask several pairs to present their dialogs to the class.

Teaching Note: You might ask students if they know how to turn off the gas, water, and electricity in their homes in case of emergency. Suggest that students find out the locations of the fuse box and other important valves and switches in their homes.

WORKBOOK

Unit 7, Page 56, Exercise 10.

FOLLOW-UP

Disconnecting Utilities: You might tell students that it is important to

notify utility companies when they move to avoid being charged for services they did not use. Ask them what information is important in arranging for services to be disconnected (new address, date of disconnection). Write their ideas on the board.

♦ Have pairs use the list on the board to create conversations about disconnecting utilities. Have several pairs present their conversations to the class.

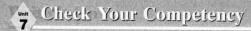
Can you use the competencies?

☐ 1. Identify rooms, furniture, and kinds of housing
☐ 2. Read for-rent ads
☐ 3. Ask for utilities to be turned on
☐ 4. Ask for simple repairs

A. Review competency I.
Look at the picture. Complete the sentences.

| kitchen   refrigerator   table |

This is the _____kitchen_____. There's a stove

and a _____refrigerator_____ in this room.

There isn't a _____table_____.

Check Up

Use competency I.
Use the sentences above to talk about the rooms in your home. Do you live in an apartment or a house?

PRESENTATION

Use any of the procedures in "Evaluation," page viii, with these pages. Record individuals' results on the Unit 7 Individual Competency Chart. Record the class's results on the Class Cumulative Competency Chart.

Check Up

B. Use competency 2.
Read the ad. Answer the questions.

1. How many bedrooms are there? _____2_____

2. How many bathrooms are there? _____1_____

3. How much is the rent? ___$550___

4. How much is the deposit? ___$200___

> **For rent:**
> 2 bdrm, 1 ba apt, furn.
> 420 Spruce Street, Apt. J.
> Near school. Pets OK.
> $550 mo plus $200 deposit.
> Call 555-6718, evenings.

C. Review competency 3. Complete the dialog.

| turned on   water |

➤ **City** ___Water___ **Company.** May I help you?

● Yes, I need the **water** ___turned on___ at my new **house.**

➤ OK. We can do it **today.**

Check Up

Use competency 3. You need the gas and electricity
turned on in your home. Use the dialog above to
call the City Gas and Electric company.

Check Up

D. Use competency 4. Your kitchen light is broken.
Complete the note to ask for repairs.

✔

| broken   electrician   light |

Dear Ms. Berger,

The ___light___ in my kitchen is ___broken___ .

Please call an ___electrician___ .

Thank you.

_____ (your signature)

FOLLOW-UP

ENGLISH IN ACTION

An Optional Cooperative Learning Project: You may want to have students create a bulletin board of housing information, which could be left up for several weeks and updated and discussed at regular intervals. Help students decide what kind of information should be included. Possibilities include information on available housing students know about, notices about used furniture and appliances for sale, names of home repair businesses students want to recommend, customer service phone numbers, and deposit information for local utility companies. It might also include the phone numbers of the Public Utilities Inquiries and Complaint lines and the local tenants' associations and/or rental arbitration boards with information about what services these agencies provide.

Students might put permanent headings on the board to organize the information and keep a supply of index cards and push pins handy for writing and posting notices. Encourage students to add any information they think will be helpful to others. Remind them to check the board for new information and remove cards with out-of-date information.

Unit 8 Overview

UNIT WARM-UP

The focus of Unit 8, "Health Care," is doctors' appointments, kinds of health care facilities, and common medical complaints and their symptoms. To stimulate a discussion, you might arrange a display of pictures depicting common illnesses and injuries. Encourage students to talk about their own experiences in visiting doctors and describing their illnesses. Have students name practices they think are important in maintaining good health.

Unit 8 Optional Materials

● Pictures depicting people with the illnesses mentioned in this unit: backache, cold, cough, earache, fever, flu, headache, sore throat, stomachache, and toothache. You might also include a picture of a pregnant woman.

● A patient information form similar to the one on page 108 on an overhead transparency.

● A real oral thermometer.

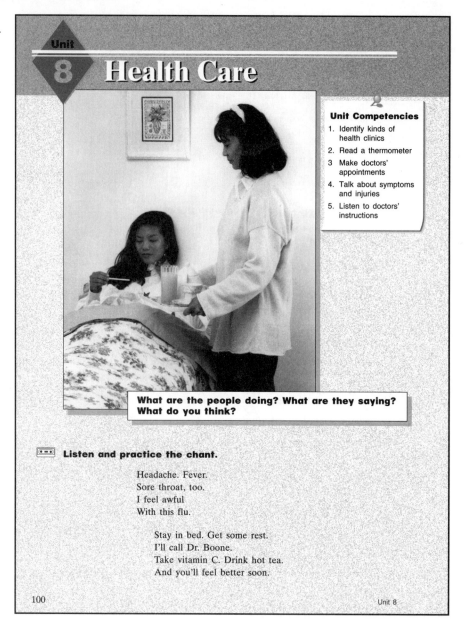

Unit 8

Health Care

Unit Competencies
1. Identify kinds of health clinics
2. Read a thermometer
3. Make doctors' appointments
4. Talk about symptoms and injuries
5. Listen to doctors' instructions

What are the people doing? What are they saying? What do you think?

Listen and practice the chant.

Headache. Fever.
Sore throat, too.
I feel awful
With this flu.

Stay in bed. Get some rest.
I'll call Dr. Boone.
Take vitamin C. Drink hot tea.
And you'll feel better soon.

100

Unit 8

COMPETENCIES (page 100)

Talk about symptoms and injuries

PREPARATION

Preteach the new language in the chant. Follow these suggestions.

● To present **headache, fever, the flu,** and **sore throat,** use pictures or pantomime. Have students repeat each word after you.

● You may also want to preteach other expressions in the chant: **I feel awful, get some rest.**

PRESENTATION

Focus attention on the photo and have students answer the questions. Encourage them to say everything they can about it. Write their ideas

on the board or restate them in acceptable English.

Present the chant. See "Presenting Chants" on page vi.

Teaching Note: You might want to explain that vitamin C is thought to help ward off colds and the flu and to reduce the symptoms of these illnesses.

WORKBOOK

Unit 8, Page 57, Exercise 1.

FOLLOW-UP

Pantomime: Have pairs of students pantomime the chant as the class says it. Continue until everyone who wants to participate has done so.

♦ Have students work in pairs to tell each other about illnesses they have experienced and what they did to get well. Have students tell each other's stories to the class.

Starting Out

A. Look and read.

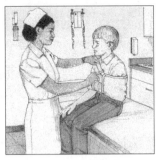

1. Ms. Garza is at City Clinic.
   She's pregnant.
   She's getting a check-up.

2. Dan is in the emergency room.
   He has a broken arm.

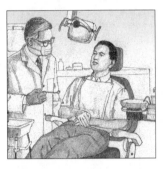

3. Mr. Li is at the dentist's office.
   He has a toothache.

4. Ms. Hill is at the doctor's office.
   She has a stomachache.

B. Answer the questions.

1. Where are the people?
2. Why are they there?
3. Where do you go when you get sick?

Unit 8   101

PREPARATION

Use pantomime, pictures depicting illnesses, and pictures of medical facilities to preteach the new language. Follow these suggestions.

● To present **stomachache, toothache,** and **broken arm,** use pictures and/or pantomime. Have students say each word after you.

● Use the picture of a pregnant woman or the picture on the page to introduce **pregnant.**

● To present **clinic, hospital, dentist's office,** and **doctor's office,** use the pictures on the Student Book page. Name each one and have students repeat. Point out that hospital emergency rooms handle urgent medical situations.

PRESENTATION

A. Have students talk about the pictures. Encourage students to say everything they can about them. Write their ideas on the board or restate them in acceptable English. Play the tape or read the captions aloud. Then have students read the captions independently.

B. Demonstrate by answering the questions about the first picture. Have students work in pairs to complete the activity. Ask several students to share their answers with the class.

WORKBOOK

Unit 8, Page 57, Exercise 2.

FOLLOW-UP

What Was It Like? Have students work in small groups to tell each other about their experiences in going to medical facilities. Who has been to an emergency room? Who has seen a dentist or a doctor? What was it like? Have groups share their conversations with the class.

♦ Have students write two or three sentences about one of their visits to a doctor, dentist, or hospital. Have volunteers read their sentences to the class.

Talk It Over

A. Gustavo Delgado is getting a check-up.
   Practice the dialog.

➤ Please get on the scale,
   Mr. Delgado.
   OK, you weigh 150 pounds.

➤ Now, let me look at your
   throat. Say "ah."
● Ahhh.
➤ OK. That looks good.

➤ Now breathe in.

➤ And now breathe out.
   Excellent. You're in very
   good health.

B. **Work with a partner. Look at the pictures in A.**
   Take turns giving the instructions.
   Do what your partner says.

102   Unit 8

PREPARATION

Use the picture of the doctor's office you used with page 101 to preteach or review the language on the page. Follow these suggestions.

● To introduce **scale**, draw a simple picture of a scale on the board. Then pantomime stepping onto a scale and weighing yourself.

PRESENTATION

A. Have students talk about the photos. Encourage students to say everything they can about them. Write their ideas on the board or restate them in acceptable English. Then present the dialog. See "Presenting Dialogs" on page vi.

Teaching Note: You might discuss the value of having regular check-ups as part of a program for staying healthy.

B. Demonstrate by asking a student to say *ah* or to breathe in. Have the student carry out the direction. Then have students complete the activity. Have them switch roles and repeat the activity.

WORKBOOK

Unit 8, Page 58, Exercise 3.

FOLLOW-UP

Doctors' Instructions: Help students make a list on the board of instructions that might be used in a doctor's office: breathe in, breathe out, turn your head, open your mouth, raise your arm, and so on. Have students work in small groups. Have group members take turns calling out instructions for the other group members to pantomime.

♦ Have students stand up. Call out a series of instructions for students to respond to as quickly as possible. Students who miss an instruction must sit down. The last student standing is the winner. You might invite students to act as callers for repeat games.

Word Bank

A. Study the vocabulary.

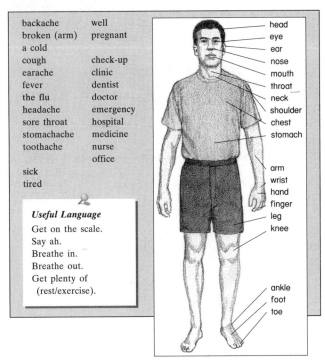

backache	well
broken (arm)	pregnant
a cold	
cough	check-up
earache	clinic
fever	dentist
the flu	doctor
headache	emergency
sore throat	hospital
stomachache	medicine
toothache	nurse
	office
sick	
tired	

Useful Language

Get on the scale.
Say ah.
Breathe in.
Breathe out.
Get plenty of
(rest/exercise).

Body labels: head, eye, ear, nose, mouth, throat, neck, shoulder, chest, stomach, arm, wrist, hand, finger, leg, knee, ankle, foot, toe

 B. Work with a partner. You're at the doctor's office. Show where it hurts. Tell where it hurts. Use words from A.

1. You have a stomachache.
2. You have a broken wrist.
3. You have a sore throat.
4. You have a headache.

 C. Work with a partner. Talk about where you go for health care. Who works there? Use words from A.

Unit 8   103

PREPARATION

Preteach or review the new vocabulary before students open their books. Use the pictures you used with pages 100 and 101. Use pantomime to introduce **tired** and **well.** Provide any reinforcement necessary. See "Reinforcing Vocabulary" on page vi.

PRESENTATION

A. Have students scan the list. Define, or have students define, any words individuals do not recognize. Provide any reinforcement necessary. See "Reinforcing Vocabulary" on page vi. Remind students that they can use this list throughout the unit to look up words, to check spelling, and to find key phrases.

B. Demonstrate by showing and telling where it hurts to have a stomachache. Have students complete the activity. Then have the class show and tell where it hurts as you name the ailments.

C. Have students complete the activity. Have several pairs of students present their dialogs to the class.

WORKBOOK

Unit 8, Pages 58–59, Exercises 4A–4C.

FOLLOW-UP

Check-Ups: Write these questions on the board: How often should people go to the doctor for check-ups? What are the benefits of getting regular check-ups? How often should you have your teeth checked? Why are dental check-ups important? Have students work in small groups to answer the questions. Have one member of each group tell the class about the group's answers.

♦ Have students work in small groups. Have each group choose one question from their discussions and make a poster illustrating the answer. Display the posters around the room.

Identify kinds of health clinics

Talk about symptoms and injuries

Listen to doctors' instructions

Listening

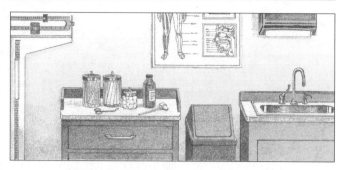

 A. Look and listen. Who do the people need to see? Circle the answer.

1. (doctor)   dentist
2. doctor   (dentist)
3. (doctor)   dentist

B. Look and listen. Complete the sentences.

| check-up   flu   stomachache |

1. David has a _____ stomachache _____.

2. Ms. Long needs a _____ check-up _____.

3. Ms. Buzek has the _____ flu _____.

About You

Listen again. What does the doctor say? Complete the sentences.

| candy   months   sleep |

1. Stop eating so much _____ candy _____.

2. Come back in six _____ months _____.

3. Get plenty of _____ sleep _____. Drink water, tea, and juice.

104   Unit 8

PREPARATION

If necessary, use the pictures you used with page 100 to review the vocabulary for describing symptoms. Use the pictures you used with page 101 to review kinds of medical facilities. Have students look at the picture on this page and discuss the kinds of things that are found in a doctor's or dentist's office. Provide any reinforcement necessary. See "Reinforcing Vocabulary" on page vi.

PRESENTATION

A. Have students read the directions for the activity. Make sure they understand what they are to do. Have students complete the activity as you play the tape or read the

Listening Transcript aloud two or more times. Check students' work.

About You **B.** Have students read the directions for the first part of the activity. Make sure they understand that they will use words from the box to complete the sentences. Have students complete the first part of the activity as you play the tape or read the Listening Transcript aloud two or more times.

Repeat the same procedure for the second part of B. Check students' work.

WORKBOOK

Unit 8, Page 60, Exercise 5.

FOLLOW-UP

An Apple a Day: Have students

work in small groups. Ask them to talk about what they eat, drink, and do to stay healthy. You might demonstrate by describing your favorite health tips: drink lots of water, eat three pieces of fruit a day, walk for twenty minutes three times a week, and so on. Have groups share their health tips with the class.

♦ Have students write their health tips on sheets of paper. They might put the tips in chart form under the headings **Food, Drink,** and **Activities.** Have volunteers show their charts to the class.

Reading

A. Look and read.

NEW CLINIC OFFERS LOW-COST HEALTH CARE

John Jones is sick. He wants to see a doctor. Where can he go?
Starting next week he can go to the new Community Health Clinic.
It opens on Monday, July 1, at 408 West 10th Street.

Community Health Clinic is not a hospital. But many doctors and
nurses work there to provide health care at a low cost.

Everyone can get excellent health care at the clinic.
These are some of the services:
• General check-ups
• Pregnancy check-ups
• Children's health care
• Non-emergency illnesses and injuries
• Treatment of many <u>minor</u> emergencies

The Community Health Clinic is having a special Health Fair Day
on July 1. You can meet the doctors and nurses, get a free blood
pressure check, and get shots for you and your children.
For information, call 555-8924.

Need list of free clinics.

B. Answer the questions. Write *yes* or *no.*

1. Is the Community Health Clinic a hospital? _____no_____

2. Do doctors work at the clinic? _____yes_____

3. Is the clinic expensive? _____no_____

4. Can you get a check-up at the clinic? _____yes_____

5. Can you go there if you have a cold or the flu? _____yes_____

 ### C. Work with a small group. Answer the questions.

1. Why do people go to health clinics? Give more than one reason.
2. Do you go to health clinics? Why or why not?

Unit 8   105

PREPARATION

If necessary, review the names of
medical facilities. Follow the instructions in "Preparation" on page 101.

PRESENTATION

A. Have students preview the
newspaper article for a few minutes
before they read it. See "Prereading"
on page vii. Encourage them to say
everything they can about the article.
Write their ideas on the board or
restate them in acceptable English.
Have students read the article
independently.

B. Have students read and answer
the questions orally and/or in writing. Have pairs of students compare
their answers.

C. Demonstrate by giving one
or two reasons why people
might go to health clinics. Have students complete the activity. Have
groups share their answers with the
class.

WORKBOOK

Unit 8, Page 60, Exercise 6.

FOLLOW-UP

Emergency or Not: Put **Emergency,
Minor Emergency,** and **Non-
Emergency** on the board. Have students brainstorm medical situations
and decide which category each situation belongs in. Have them talk
about the kinds of actions medical
emergencies require (calling 911,
going to emergency room) and the

kinds of actions minor emergencies
and non-emergencies require (going
to a health clinic, making an appointment with a doctor).

♦ Write **Calling 911** on the board.
Have students brainstorm a list of
situations that warrant calling 911.
Then have students talk about the
information callers should be prepared to give when making a 911
call. Take notes on the board.

Teaching Note: Remind students
that a 911 call from a pay phone does
not require a coin deposit.

Talk about symptoms and injuries

Structure Base

A. Study the examples.

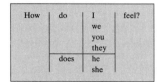

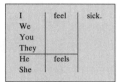

How	do	I we you they	feel?
	does	he she	

I We You They	feel	sick.
He She	feels	

B. Ms. Davidov and her daughter are at the doctor's office. Complete the dialog. Use the words from A.

➤ Hi, Ms. Davidov. How _____do_____ you _____feel_____?

● I _____feel_____ fine, Dr. Agoyo. But Sophia is sick.

➤ Oh, no. How _____does_____ she _____feel_____?

● She _____feels_____ terrible. She has a stomachache.

➤ Come here, Sophia. Let's see what we can do for you.

C. Work with a small group. Talk about how you feel. Follow the examples in A.

PREPARATION

If necessary, review the vocabulary in the language boxes with students before they open their books. Follow the instructions in "Preparation" on pages 100 and 103.

PRESENTATION

A. Have students read the language boxes independently. Have students use the words in the language boxes to say as many sentences as they can. Explain to students that they can refer to the language boxes throughout the unit to check or review sentence patterns.

B. Demonstrate by doing the first item on the board. Have students complete the activity. Have students read their completed sentences aloud while the other students check their own answers.

C. Brainstorm with students a list of words that could be used to describe how people feel: **weak, strong, so-so, awful, better, worse, cold, hot,** and so on. Write the words on the board. Demonstrate by asking several students how they feel. Have students complete the activity. Have several students tell the class how they feel.

D. Study the examples.

I	have	the flu.
We		
You		
They		
He	has	
She		

E. Look at the pictures. Complete the sentences.
Use the words in D.

She has _____ a **stomachache.**

He has _____ a **fever.**

They have _____ the **flu.**

She has _____ a **broken arm.**

F. Work with a small group.
You don't feel well. What's the matter?
Tell your group. Follow the sentences in E.

PRESENTATION

D. Follow the procedure in A.

E. Follow the procedure in B.

F. Demonstrate by saying, *I don't feel well. I have a (backache).* Have students complete the activity. Have several students tell the class what their imaginary ailments are.

WORKBOOK

Unit 8, Pages 61–62, Exercises 7A–7B.

FOLLOW-UP

Role-Play: Display the pictures showing different illnesses. Have pairs or small groups of students choose one picture and use it to cre-ate and role-play a conversation like the one in B. Have volunteers present their role-plays to the class.

♦ With students' help, write a list of illnesses and injuries on the board. Have students use the list to play a memory game. Have them sit in a semicircle facing the list on the board. Ask one student, *What's the matter?* That student chooses an ailment and replies, *I have a (cold).* Ask another student, *What's the matter?* That student chooses an ailment and answers, *I have a (broken arm). She has a (cold).* Continue questioning students until a student can't remember all the ailments. Start the game over if time allows.

Talk about symptoms and injuries

Write It Down

**A. You don't feel well.
You go to the Community Health Clinic.
Complete the form. Write about yourself.**

About You

Community Health Clinic
Patient Information Form

✚ CHC

Name ___ Answers will vary. ___

Address _____ Telephone Number _____

Date of Birth _____ Age ____ Male ____ Female ____

Who can we call in an emergency? *The answ. to who is a person*

Name _____

Telephone Number _____

What are your symptoms? Check here. (✓) *The answer to what is the name of a person or thing.*

_____ backache   _____ headache

_____ cough   _____ sore throat

_____ earache   _____ stomachache

_____ fever   _____ other (Write here.) _____

Answer *yes* or *no*.

Are you pregnant? _____

Have you ever been in the hospital? _____

If yes, why? _____

Do you exercise? _____

Do you take any medicine? _____

If yes, what medicine? _____

Signature _____ Date _____

108   Unit 8

PREPARATION
Display the transparency of the patient information form. Explain that such forms help doctors and dentists find out important information about new patients. To review describing symptoms, follow the instructions in "Preparation" on page 100. Discuss the meaning of **exercise,** if necessary.

PRESENTATION
Culture Note: You might explain that doctors often request that patients come early for their first visits to fill out forms. A medical history and information about insurance are usually requested.

About You Have students talk about the form. Write their ideas on the board or restate them in acceptable English. Have students complete the activity independently. Check students' work.

WORKBOOK
Unit 8, Page 62, Exercise 8.

FOLLOW-UP
Important Medical Information:
Have students talk about the importance of knowing their medical histories and those of their children and other family members. Take notes on the board about the important information everyone should know: the name and address of the person to contact in case of emergency, past

childhood illnesses (measles, chicken pox), any serious illnesses or surgeries, any allergies to medication, and so on.

♦ Give students index cards. Help them use the list on the board as a guide to write their own medical information and/or medical information about family members on the cards. Suggest that they keep the cards as permanent records to use when they visit a medical facility.

One To One   Student A

I. Practice the dialog.

➤ What's the matter with **Calvin?**
● **He** has a **backache.**

Calvin/Dee/Mei-hua

**2. What's the matter with them? Ask Student B.
Follow the dialog in I. Write the information.**   *Use vocab. p.103*

a. Calvin ___has a___   b. Dee ___has a___   c. Mei-hua ___has a___

___backache___ .   ___cold___ .   ___fever___ .

**3. What's the matter with them?
Tell Student B. Follow the dialog in I.**

   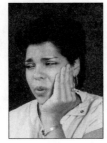   

a. Albert   b. Marilyn   c. Yong-shik

4. Switch roles. Turn to page 110. Complete 2 and 3.

**5. Talk with a partner.
What should the people do?
Who should go to the dentist?
Who should go to the doctor?
Who should stay home and rest?**

Unit 8   109

PREPARATION

If necessary, review the vocabulary for discussing symptoms and illnesses. Follow the instructions in "Preparation" on page 100.

PRESENTATION

Teaching Note: For more information on these pages, see "One to One" on page vii.

1. Have students find partners. Assign the roles of A and B. Explain that Student A looks only at page A (page 109) and Student B only at page B (page 110). Have them turn to the appropriate pages. Then present the dialog. See "Presenting Dialogs" on page vi.

2. Have students read the directions independently. Model the activity with a student. Then have students complete the activity.

3. Have students read the directions independently and complete the activity.

4. Have students read the directions and complete the activity. You may want students to switch partners at this time, too. Check students' answers for both pages.

WORKBOOK

Unit 8, Page 63, Exercise 9.

FOLLOW-UP

Ways To Feel Better: Though it is important to emphasize that many conditions require a doctor's or a dentist's care, you might discuss with students their ways of handling minor ailments. Help students make a list of minor ailments on the board, such as a headache, cold, stomachache, or a small cut. Ask students to talk about ways they handle these complaints.

♦ Have students choose one of the minor ailments on the board and write two or three sentences on how they would handle it. Have volunteers read their sentences to the class.

Talk about symptoms and injuries

One To One   **Student B**

I. **Practice the dialog.**

➤ What's the matter with **Calvin?**
● He has a **backache.**

 2. **What's the matter with them?**
Tell Student A. Follow the dialog in I.

a. Calvin   b. Dee   c. Mei-hua

 3. **What's the matter with them? Ask Student A.**
Follow the dialog in I. Write the information.

a. Albert <u>has a</u>   b. Marilyn <u>has a</u>   c. Yong-shik <u>has a</u>

<u>headache</u>.   <u>toothache</u>.   <u>sore throat</u>.

4. **Switch roles. Turn to page 109. Complete 2 and 3.**

5. **Talk with a partner.**
What should the people do?
Who should go to the dentist?
Who should go to the doctor?
Who should stay home and rest?

110   Unit 8

PRESENTATION

Follow the instructions on page 109.

Extension

**A. Study the thermometers.
Answer the questions.**

Normal temperature

John's temperature

1. What's normal temperature? ___98.6___ degrees

2. What's John's temperature? ___102___ degrees

3. Does John have a fever? ___yes___

 **B. John is calling the doctor's office.
He needs to make an appointment.
Practice the dialog.**

● Good morning. **Dr. Thien's** office.
➤ Hello. This is **John Kraft.** I need to make an appointment.
● What's the matter?
➤ I have a **sore throat and a 102 degree fever.**
● Can you come in **this afternoon** at **4:30?**
➤ Yes, I can.
● All right, **Mr. Kraft.** The doctor will see you then.

**C. Work with a partner.
You have a fever.
Read your temperature.
Make a doctor's appointment for yourself.
Use the dialog in B.**

PREPARATION

Draw a simple thermometer on the board and mark 98.6 degrees. Explain that a thermometer measures body temperature and that body temperature can be an excellent indicator of good health or illness. Model taking your temperature with a real thermometer.

Teaching Note: You might explain that on the Celsius scale normal body temperature is 37 degrees. You might point out that 98.6 is said *98 point 6.*

PRESENTATION

A. Have students look at the two thermometers. Encourage them to say everything they can about them. Write their ideas on the board or restate them in acceptable English. Have students read the directions and complete the activity. Check students' work.

B. Have students read the directions. Then present the dialog. See "Presenting Dialogs" on page vi.

C. Demonstrate with a student by using the dialog in B to make a doctor's appointment. Have students complete the activity. Ask several pairs of students to present their dialogs to the class.

WORKBOOK

Unit 8, Page 64, Exercise 10.

FOLLOW-UP

Before Calling the Doctor: Have students work in small groups. Ask them to talk about the kinds of information they should have ready when making a doctor's appointment. Have groups report their findings to the class.

◆ Have students write lists of things they need to know when making a doctor's appointment. Have students post their lists around the room.

Can you use the competencies?

- ☐ 1. Identify kinds of health clinics
- ☐ 2. Read a thermometer
- ☐ 3. Make doctors' appointments
- ☐ 4. Talk about symptoms and injuries
- ☐ 5. Listen to doctors' instructions

 **A. Use competency I. Where are they?
Complete the sentences.**

dentist's office	doctor's office	emergency room

 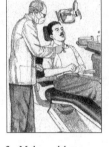 

1. Leah has a sore throat. She's at

   <u>the doctor's office</u>.

2. Mohamed has a toothache. He's at

   <u>the dentist's office</u>.

3. Mr. Robledo has a broken arm. He's at

   <u>the emergency room</u>.

 **B. Use competency 2. Read Jill's temperature.
Answer the questions.**

Jill's temperature

1. What's Jill's temperature? <u>101</u> degrees
2. Normal temperature is 98.6 degrees.
   Does Jill have a fever? <u>yes</u>

112   Unit 8

PRESENTATION

Use any of the procedures in "Evaluation," page viii, with these pages. For exercise D, play the tape or read the Listening Transcript aloud two or more times. Record individuals' results on the Unit 8 Individual Competency Chart. Record the class's results on the Class Cumulative Competency Chart.

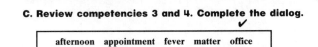

C. Review competencies 3 and 4. Complete the dialog. ✔

afternoon appointment fever matter office

➤ Good morning. Dr. Hansen's _____office_____ .

● Hello. This is **Jill Mason.** I want to make an _____appointment_____ .

➤ What's the _____matter_____ ?

● **I have a** high _____fever_____ .

➤ Can you come in this _____afternoon_____ at 4:00?

● **Yes, I can. Thanks.**

 Use competencies 3 and 4. Use the dialog above to make a doctor's appointment for yourself.

 D. Use competency 5. Look and listen. What does the doctor say to do? Number the pictures from 1–5.

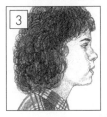

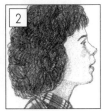

FOLLOW-UP

ENGLISH IN ACTION

An Optional Cooperative Learning Project: You may want to have students work together to create a class directory of local health care facilities. Help them decide what information to include about each place: name and address, hours of operation, phone numbers for emergencies, appointments, and questions about billing, access by public transportation, payment policies, and insurance requirements. Have a small group of students collect information about each facility. Help students decide on an organizational scheme and put their information together in a notebook. Suggest that they include a local map that indicates where each facility is located. Remind students to use the directory when they or their families need medical care; they might report to the class on how the directory helped them and add any new information they think would be helpful to other students.

Unit 9 Overview

UNIT WARM-UP

The focus of Unit 9, "Employment," is kinds of jobs, job applications, and interviews. To stimulate a discussion, you might display photographs or pictures of people performing different kinds of jobs. Identify the jobs, if necessary. Ask students what jobs they are doing now. Invite them to discuss their experiences finding work in the U.S.

Unit 9 Optional Materials

● Labeled pictures of different occupations being performed by both women and men, such as child care worker, mechanic, shoe repair person, gardener, cab/bus driver, cook, house painter, housekeeper, and plumber.

● A real employment application form (if possible, on an overhead transparency).

● Copies of help-wanted ads from newspapers.

● Pictures of hazardous work situations, such as construction sites and electrical transformers.

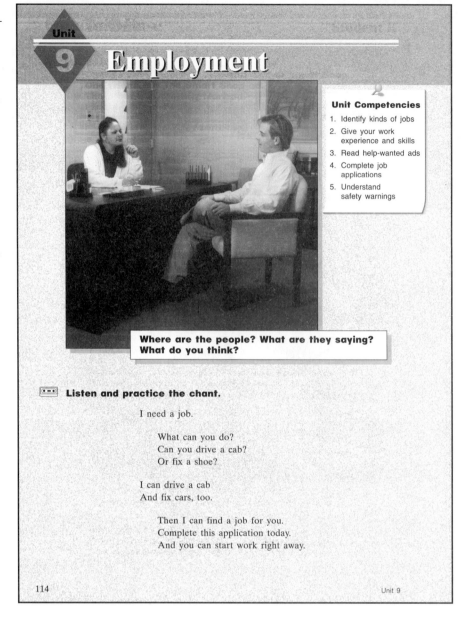

Unit 9 Employment

Unit Competencies
1. Identify kinds of jobs
2. Give your work experience and skills
3. Read help-wanted ads
4. Complete job applications
5. Understand safety warnings

Where are the people? What are they saying? What do you think?

Listen and practice the chant.

I need a job.

What can you do?
Can you drive a cab?
Or fix a shoe?

I can drive a cab
And fix cars, too.

Then I can find a job for you.
Complete this application today.
And you can start work right away.

114   Unit 9

COMPETENCIES (page 114)

Identify kinds of jobs
Give your work experience and skills

PREPARATION

Use pictures of different occupations and the application form to preteach the new language in the chant. Follow these suggestions.

● Use pictures to preteach **cab, driver,** and **fix.** Say the words and have students repeat.

● To preteach **application,** show an employment application or an overhead transparency of one. Explain that employers ask job seekers to complete applications, which ask for information about the job seeker.

PRESENTATION

Focus attention on the photo and have students answer the questions. Encourage them to say everything they can about it. Write their ideas on the board or restate them in acceptable English.

Present the chant. See "Presenting Chants" on page vi.

WORKBOOK

Unit 9, Page 65, Exercise 1.

FOLLOW-UP

Work Experience: Have students work in small groups to discuss jobs they are interested in as well as those they would like to learn more about. Have individuals report their group's

jobs to the class.

◆ Using the information from the previous activity, the class can create a jobs chart, listing all the occupations discussed by the class. Post the chart on a bulletin board.

Starting Out

COMPETENCIES (page 115)

Identify kinds of jobs

Give your work experience
and skills

A. People are interviewing for jobs. Look and read.

➤ Can you paint houses, Pedro?
● Yes, I can. I was a painter in my country.
➤ How long were you a painter?
● For 23 years.

➤ Can you cook, Mu-tan?
● Yes, I can. I was a cook in my country.
➤ How long were you a cook?
● From 1986 to 1988.

B. Answer the questions.

1. What can the people do? What did they do in their countries?
2. What jobs can you do? What did you do in your country?

Unit 9   115

PREPARATION

Use pictures depicting occupations you used with page 114 to preteach the new language. Follow these suggestions.

● To present **house painter** and **cook,** hold up pictures showing each activity or occupation. Say the words and have students repeat.

● To present **interview,** write the word on the board. Tell students that an interview is a conversation between an employer and a job seeker to see if the job seeker can do the job and if he or she wants the job. Have students repeat the word after you.

Teaching Note: You may want to explain that making a good first impression in a job interview is important. Some points to consider are: clean dress, promptness, direct eye contact, and good posture.

PRESENTATION

A. Have students talk about the photographs. Have them say everything they can about the photos. Write their ideas on the board or restate them in acceptable English. Play the tape or read the captions aloud while students follow along in their books. Then present the dialogs. See "Presenting Dialogs" on page vi.

B. Demonstrate by answering the first question on the board. Have students complete the activity independently. Ask several students to share their answers with the class.

WORKBOOK

Unit 9, Page 65, Exercise 2.

FOLLOW-UP

Job Tasks: Have students work in small groups to brainstorm what tasks are involved in doing the jobs of a house painter and a cook. Members of the groups can pantomime the tasks for the class. Class members can figure out the tasks and occupations.

◆ Using the information from the previous activity, students can list the job-related tasks for each of the occupations. Individuals can share their lists with the class.

Talk It Over

A. Look and read.

1. cab driver   2. gardener   3. plumber

4. housekeeper   5. child care worker   6. mechanic

B. Practice the dialog.

➤ My name is Ricardo. I'm looking for a job.
● Can you drive a cab?
➤ Yes, I can.
● Do you have any experience?
➤ Yes, I was a cab driver for five years.

C. Talk to other students. Write the students' names.

1. _Ricardo_____ can drive a cab. *cab driver*
2. _____ can grow plants. *gardener*
3. _____ can fix sinks. *plumber*
4. _____ can clean houses and make beds. *housekeeper*
5. _____ can take care of children. *child care worker*
6. _____ can paint houses. *house painter*

116   Unit 9

PREPARATION

Use pictures depicting different occupations to preteach or review the language on the page. Follow these suggestions.

● To present **cab driver, gardener, plumber, housekeeper, child care worker,** and **mechanic,** hold up pictures showing each occupation. Name the occupations and have students repeat.

● To present **grow plants, fix sinks, clean houses, make beds, take care of children, paint houses, cook, fix cars,** and **drive,** use pictures to tie these tasks to occupations. Have students repeat the tasks.

● Present the question **Do you have any experience?** Give a personal example of your length of experience on a job.

PRESENTATION

A. Have students talk about the photographs. Encourage them to say everything they can about them. Write their ideas on the board or restate them in acceptable English. Then have students read the captions independently.

B. Play the tape or read the dialog aloud while students follow along in their books. See "Presenting Dialogs" on page vi.

C. Have students work in small groups to complete the activity. Suggest that they might use part of the dialog in B to gather information.

Have volunteers share their lists with the class.

WORKBOOK

Unit 9, Page 66, Exercise 3.

FOLLOW-UP

✳ **Names of Occupations:** Using the job descriptions in C in the Student Book, have students name the occupations that go with the tasks. For example, *Ricardo can drive a cab. Ricardo is a cab driver.*

◆ Students can use the information from the previous activity to make posters showing different occupations and job tasks. Students can label their posters and display them on a bulletin board.

Word Bank

Identify kinds of jobs

Give your work experience
and skills

A. Study the vocabulary.

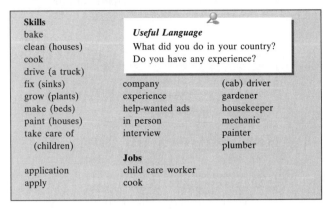

Skills
bake
clean (houses)
cook
drive (a truck)

Useful Language
What did you do in your country?
Do you have any experience?

fix (sinks)   company   (cab) driver
grow (plants)   experience   gardener
make (beds)   help-wanted ads housekeeper
paint (houses)   in person   mechanic
take care of   interview   painter
   (children)   plumber

Jobs
application   child care worker
apply   cook

 B. Use words from A to complete the sentences.

1. A gardener _____grows_____ plants.

2. A housekeeper _____cleans_____ houses.

3. A painter _____paints_____ houses and other buildings.

4. A mechanic _____fixes_____ cars, buses, or trucks.

5. A child care worker _____takes care of_____ children.

6. A plumber _____fixes_____ sinks.

7. A bus driver _____drives_____ a bus.

**C. Work with a small group. Talk about jobs. What can you do?
What job do you want?**

Unit 9   117

PREPARATION

Preteach or review the new vocabulary before students open their books. Give special attention to **bake, apply, company, help-wanted ads**, and **in person,** by using the examples from the employment application or overhead transparency, pictures, and help-wanted ads from the newspaper. Say the words and have students repeat them. Provide any reinforcement necessary. See "Reinforcing Vocabulary" on page vi.

PRESENTATION

A. Have students scan the list. Define, or have other students define, any words individuals do not

recognize. Provide any reinforcement necessary. See "Reinforcing Vocabulary" on page vi. Remind students that they can use this list throughout the unit to look up words, to check spelling, and to find key phrases.

B. Have students read the instructions. Demonstrate by doing the first item. Have students complete the activity independently. Check students' work.

C. Demonstrate by describing the job you would do if you weren't a teacher. Have students work in small groups. Have them talk about the jobs they would like to have. Have several groups repeat their conversations for the class.

WORKBOOK

Unit 9, Pages 66–67, Exercises 4A–4D.

FOLLOW-UP

✳ **Job-Related Tasks:** Students can work in small groups to brainstorm additional job-related tasks for the *Occup.* occupations on the Student Book *wksht.* page. Individuals can share their tasks with the class.

♦ Using the information from the previous activity, the class can make a master list of job tasks for each of the occupations. Post lists on a bulletin board.

Identify kinds of jobs

Give your work experience
 and skills

Listening

**A. Three people are interviewing for jobs.
Look and listen. What were their jobs before?
Circle the jobs in column A.**

	A Job	**B** Skill
1.	bus driver	fix buses
	(mechanic)	drive buses
	gardener	(fix cars)
2.	(cook)	drive a bus
	mechanic	(cook)
	housekeeper	bake cakes
3.	(cab driver)	cook in a hotel
	truck driver	drive a truck
	mechanic	(drive a bus)

**Listen again. What can they do now?
Circle the skills in column B.**

**B. Soo-ha Lee is calling about a job. Look and listen.
Read the questions. Circle the answers.**

1. What job is Soo-ha calling about? (gardener) painter
2. How long was she a gardener? 3 years (3 months)
3. Can Soo-ha grow plants? (yes) no
4. Can she take care of trees? yes (no)

**C. Work with a small group.
Do you think Soo-ha will get the job?
Why or why not?**

Transcript.p.150

118   Unit 9

PREPARATION

If necessary, use the pictures of occupations to review the vocabulary on this page.

PRESENTATION

A. Have students read the directions for the first part of the activity. Make sure students understand that they will listen and circle the correct words in column A. Have students listen and complete the first part of the activity independently as you play the tape or read the Listening Transcript aloud two or more times. Repeat the same procedure with the second part of A. Make sure students understand that they are to circle the correct words in Column B. Check students' work.

B. Have students read the directions. Make sure they understand that they will circle the correct answer. Have students listen and complete the activity independently as you play the tape or read the Listening Transcript two or more times. Check students' work.

C. Have students work in small groups to complete the activity. Have someone from each group say whether they think Soo-ha will get the job and why.

WORKBOOK

Unit 9, Page 68, Exercise 5.

FOLLOW-UP

Transferable Skills: Have each student make a list of the work he or she has done and what the duties were. Then have students meet in small groups. Have each member of the group share his or her experience, so the rest of the group can brainstorm different jobs the student could do. Have volunteers share their list of possible jobs with the class.

♦ Have students make charts of the skills they have used in jobs they've held. Have students work in small groups to brainstorm different jobs each student can do. Have volunteers share their job possibilities with the class.

Reading

**A. Many businesses advertise jobs in newspapers.
Ads for jobs are called help-wanted ads. Look and read.**

Twin Cities Times — Section C

HELP WANTED

(A.) Cooks wanted.
Apply in person at
Midnight Diner,
170 Collins Avenue.

(B.) Child Care Workers.
Experience necessary.
Apply now. Send letter.
Twin Cities Day Care,
1000 W. Market Street.

(C.) WANTED: Cab drivers.
No experience necessary.
Must have driver's license.
Apply in person at
Twin Cities Cab Company,
833 First Street.
Monday to Friday, 8 to 5.

(D.) GARDENER needed.
Experience necessary.
Call 555-3233.

(E.) MECHANIC NEEDED
Start immediately.
Must have 3 years' experience.
Apply in person.
Hank's Garage, 111 Main Street.

(F.) WANTED: Housekeeper
No experience necessary.
Call 555-4892 for an appointment.

About You

B. Answer the questions about the ads. Write the letters.

1. Which ads say you must apply in person?   A, C, E

2. Which ads say to call?   D, F

3. Which ads say you need experience?   B, D, E

4. Which ad says to send a letter?   B

5. Which ad is for cab drivers?   C

About You

**C. Work with a partner. Talk about the ads.
Would you apply for one of the jobs?
Why or why not?**

Unit 9   119

PREPARATION

If necessary, preteach or review the vocabulary used on this page. Use the pictures of occupations, the employment application or overhead transparency, and the help-wanted ads.

PRESENTATION

A. Have students preview the ads before they read them. See "Pre-reading" on page vii. Then have them read the ads independently.

About You B. Demonstrate by answering the first question on the board. Have the students read and answer the questions in writing. Have several students say their answers aloud while the other students check their own answers.

C. Demonstrate by saying which job you would apply for. Have students find partners, read the directions, and complete the activity. Partners can share their answers with the class.

WORKBOOK

Unit 9, Page 68, Exercise 6.

FOLLOW-UP

Reading Want Ads: Distribute want-ad sections of newspapers to small groups of students. Have students find ads for jobs for which they might be qualified. Have individuals share their ads with the class and tell why they are qualified for the jobs.

♦ Using the ads from the previous activity, have students write questions they would ask about the jobs in the ads. Volunteers can share their ads and questions with the class.

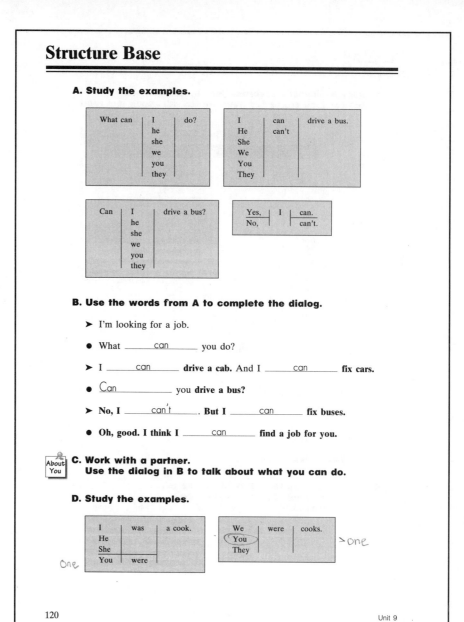

Structure Base

A. Study the examples.

What can	I	do?
	he	
	she	
	we	
	you	
	they	

		drive a bus.
I	can	
He	can't	
She		
We		
You		
They		

Can	I	drive a bus?
	he	
	she	
	we	
	you	
	they	

Yes,	I	can.
No,		can't.

B. Use the words from A to complete the dialog.

➤ I'm looking for a job.

● What _____can_____ you do?

➤ I _____can_____ **drive a cab.** And I _____can_____ **fix cars.**

● Can _____ **you drive a bus?**

➤ No, I _____can't_____ . But I _____can_____ **fix buses.**

● Oh, good. I think I _____can_____ **find a job for you.**

About You

C. Work with a partner.
Use the dialog in B to talk about what you can do.

D. Study the examples.

I	was	a cook.	One
He			
She			
You	were		

We	were	cooks.	>One
(You)			
They			

120   Unit 9

PREPARATION

If necessary, preteach or review the
vocabulary in the language boxes
with students before they open their
books.

PRESENTATION

A. Have students read the language
boxes independently. Have students
use the words in the boxes to say as
many sentences as they can. Explain
to students that they can refer to the
language boxes throughout the unit
to check or review sentence patterns.

B. Demonstrate by doing the first
item on the board. Have students
complete the activity. Have several
students read their sentences aloud
while the other students check their
own answers.

About You **C.** Demonstrate by having a
student ask you questions about
your skills. Have students complete
the activity in pairs. Have several
pairs share their conversations with
the class.

D. Follow the procedure in A.

E. Use the words from D to complete the sentences.

➤ What did you do in your country, Katya?

● I _____was_____ a painter.

➤ How interesting. I _____was_____ a bus driver.

● Really? What about your brother?
Was he a bus driver, too?

➤ Yes, he _____was_____. We _____were_____ bus drivers
in the same city.

 F. Work with a small group.
Talk about what you did in your country.
Follow the examples in D.

G. Study the examples.

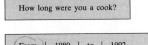 How long were you a cook?

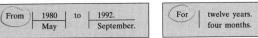

From | 1980 | to | 1992.   For | twelve years.
   May | | September.   four months.

H. Use the words from G to complete the dialog.

➤ I was **a mechanic** in my country.

● Really? _____How long_____ were you **a mechanic**?

➤ __From__ **1976 to 1986.**

● Oh, ____for____ **ten years. That's a long time.**

➤ Yes. I liked it. _____How long_____ were you **a gardener**?

● __For__ **two years.** __From__ **1991 to 1993.**

 I. Work with a partner.
Use the dialog in H to talk about yourself.

Unit 9   121

PRESENTATION

E. Follow the procedure in B.

 F. Follow the procedure in C.

G. Follow the procedure in A.

H. Follow the procedure in B.

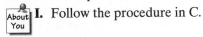 **I.** Follow the procedure in C.

WORKBOOK

Unit 9, Pages 69–70, Exercises
7A–7C.

FOLLOW-UP

✳Twenty Questions: Write the names
of jobs on slips of paper and give one
to each student. Ask a student to
stand in front of the class and answer
questions about his or her job. Class
members may ask the student only

yes/no questions, such as *Can you
cook? Can you drive a cab?* The class
can ask up to twenty questions to try
to identify the person's job. The student who correctly figures out the
job first becomes the next to answer
questions. Continue until everyone
in the class has had a chance to
answer.

♦ Using the format from the previous activity, have students write their
names and one question each on
slips of paper. Collect all the slips
and give them to the person who will
answer the questions. That person
writes **yes** or **no** on each slip and
returns them to the appropriate students. Class members analyze the
questions and answers together to
figure out the person's job. After the

job has been identified, choose
another person to answer questions.
Continue with additional students.

Write It Down

A. To apply for a job, you complete a job application. Complete the application. Write about yourself.

APPLICATION FOR EMPLOYMENT

PERSONAL INFORMATION

Name _Answers will vary._

Address _____

_____

Telephone _____ Social Security Number _____

What job are you applying for?

_____

WORK EXPERIENCE

Job _____ Company _____

Address _____

Telephone _____ How long were you at this job? _____

Job _____ Company _____

Address _____

Telephone _____ How long were you at this job? _____

READ AND SIGN
The above information is true and correct.

_____ _____

Signature   Date

PREPARATION

If necessary, review the vocabulary for this page. Follow the instructions in "Preparation" on page 117.

• You may want to discuss the purpose of a job application before students open their books. Explain that employers want to know about an interviewee's educational background, previous work experience, references, and reasons for leaving previous jobs.

• To introduce filling out the job application, use the overhead transparency of a blank employment application and fill in a few of the blanks with information about yourself or a fictitious person. Review the vocabulary on the form by reading the form aloud and having students repeat unfamiliar words after you.

PRESENTATION

A. Have students look at the application form. Encourage them to say everything they can about it. Write their ideas on the board or restate them in acceptable English. Have students complete the activity independently. Have volunteers read their applications to the class.

WORKBOOK

Unit 9, Page 71, Exercise 8.

FOLLOW-UP

Work History: Have students make lists of their past educational experience, the jobs they had in the past, their employers, why they left jobs, and descriptions of their skills and training. Collect the profiles, check them, and return them to students. Tell students that they now have detailed accounts of their work histories that they can take with them when they apply for jobs.

♦ Have students work independently to create blank job application forms. Have them exchange forms and fill out each other's applications, using their profiles from the previous activity. Ask volunteers to read their completed applications to the class.

One To One
Student A

I. Practice the dialog.

➤ **Antonio** needs a job.
● What can **he** do?
➤ **He** can **fix sinks**.
● **Acme Plumbing** needs a **plumber. He** can apply there.

2. These people need jobs. Tell Student B.
Follow the dialog in I. Write the answers.

Name:	a. Antonio	b. Jane	c. Dae Soo
Skills:	fix sinks	paint houses	cook and bake
Business:	Acme Plumbing	Pat's Painters	Kathy's Restaurant
Job:	plumber	painter	breakfast cook

 3. Read the ads. Follow the dialog in I.
Help Student B find jobs for people.

HELP WANTED

BUS DRIVERS NEEDED
Must have driver's license.
Call City Bus Company,
555-8327, for appointment.

Wanted:
Child Care Workers
Apply in person.
Happy Child Center.

ANTHONY'S GARAGE
needs a mechanic.
Experience necessary.
Apply in person.
231 Market Sreet.

4. Switch roles. Turn to page 124. Complete 2 and 3.

Unit 9   123

Identify kinds of jobs

Give your work experience
and skills

Read help-wanted ads

PREPARATION

If necessary, review the vocabulary for occupations and job related tasks. Follow the instructions in "Preparation" on page 116.

PRESENTATION

Teaching Note: For more information on these pages, see "One to One" on page vii.

1. Have students find partners. Assign the roles of A and B. Explain that Student A looks only at page A (page 123) and Student B only at page B (page 124). Have them turn to the appropriate pages. Then present the dialog. See "Presenting Dialogs" on page vi.

2. Have students read the directions independently. Model the activity with a student. Then have students complete the activity.

3. Have students read the directions independently and complete the activity.

4. Have students read the directions and complete the activity. You may want students to switch partners at this time, too. Check students' answers for both pages.

WORKBOOK

Unit 9, Page 72, Exercise 9.

FOLLOW-UP

Help-Wanted Ads: Distribute want-ad sections of newspapers to small groups of students. Students can choose occupations from the Student Book page and find ads for those occupations in the newspapers. Students can share their ads with the class.

♦ Using the ads from the previous activity, students can choose a job for each occupation that they feel is the best job. Volunteers can share their ads and reasons for choosing the jobs with the class.

Identify kinds of jobs

Give your work experience
and skills

Read help-wanted ads

One To One Student B

I. Practice the dialog.

➤ **Antonio** needs a job.
● What can **he** do?
➤ **He** can **fix sinks.**
● **Acme Plumbing** needs a **plumber. He** can apply there.

 2. Read the ads. Follow the dialog in I.
Help Student A find jobs for people.

HELP WANTED

Wanted: Plumber.
Apply at Acme Plumbing,
750 North Main Street,
between 8 and 12.

Kathy's Restaurant
needs a breakfast cook.
Apply in person
Monday to Friday at
3212 18th Street.

Painter wanted.
Must have experience.
Apply at Pat's Painters,
320 Jones Street.

3. These people need jobs. Tell Student A.
Follow the dialog in I. Write the answers.

Name:	a. Li-hua	b. Derek	c. Henka
Skills:	take care of children	fix cars	drive a bus
Business:	Happy Child Center	Anthony's Garage	City Bus Company
Job:	child care worker	mechanic	bus driver

4. Switch roles. Turn to page 123. Complete 2 and 3.

124 Unit 9

PRESENTATION

Follow the instructions on page 123.

Extension

A. These are safety warning signs. Look and read.

1.
No Smoking

2.
High Voltage
KEEP OUT

3.
HARD HAT
AREA

**B. Look at the pictures.
Are the people following the warnings? Write *yes* or *no*.**

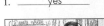

1. _____ yes _____ 　　　2. _____ no _____

3. _____ yes _____ 　　　4. _____ no _____

Unit 9

125

PREPARATION

● Hold up pictures of places where safety warnings would be posted and review the vocabulary for **hard-hat area, no smoking,** and **high-voltage.** Write the terms on the board, say the terms, and have students repeat them after you.

PRESENTATION

A. Have students talk about the pictures. Encourage them to say everything they can about them. Write their ideas on the board or restate them in acceptable English. Have students discuss where they would see such warnings.

B. Demonstrate by answering the question about the first picture. Have students look at the pic-

tures and write their answers to the questions. Check students' work.

WORKBOOK

Unit 9, Page 72, Exercise 10.

FOLLOW-UP

Warning Signs: Have students work in small groups to list warning signs they have seen in the community. Have them list the warnings and likely locations for the signs. Volunteers can share their information with the class.

♦ Using the information from the previous activity, students can make posters showing warning signs. Individuals can present their posters to the class and tell where the signs would be seen.

Check Your Competency

Can you use the competencies?

- ☐ 1. Identify kinds of jobs
- ☐ 2. Give your work experience and skills
- ☐ 3. Read help-wanted ads
- ☐ 4. Complete job applications
- ☐ 5. Understand safety warnings

Check Up

A. Use competency I.
Complete the sentences.
Write the letter.

1. A plumber __d__.
2. A painter __a__.
3. A gardener __c__.
4. A bus driver __e__.
5. A child care worker __b__.

a. paints houses
b. takes care of children
c. grows plants
✔ d. fixes sinks
e. drives a bus

B. Review competency 2. Complete the dialog.

✔

can cook do experience

➤ What can you _____do_____?

● I _____can_____ cook.

➤ Do you have _____experience_____?

● Yes. I was a _____cook_____ in my country.

Check Up

Use competency 2.
Use the dialog in B to talk about yourself.

PRESENTATION

Use any of the procedures in "Evaluation," page viii, with these pages. Record individuals' results on the Unit 9 Individual Competency Chart. Record the class's results on the Class Cumulative Competency Chart.

**C. Use competency 3. Read the help-wanted ad.
Answer the questions.**

1. What's the job? _____mechanic_____

2. Do you need experience? _____yes_____

3. Can you call to apply? _____no_____

> **MECHANIC needed.**
> Must have experience.
> Apply in person at
> 8601 Park Street.
> Monday to Friday

D. Use competency 4. Complete the job application.

APPLICATION FOR EMPLOYMENT

PERSONAL INFORMATION	WORK EXPERIENCE
Name _Answers will vary._	Job _____
Address _____	Company _____
_____	Address _____
Telephone _____	Telephone _____
Social Security Number	How long were you at this job? _____

**E. Use competency 5. Look at the pictures.
Are the people following the warning signs?
Write yes or no.**

1. _____no_____   2. _____yes_____   3. _____no_____

FOLLOW-UP

ENGLISH IN ACTION

An Optional Cooperative Learning Project: You may want to offer students a chance to improve their interviewing skills. Ask a representative from the Human Resources department of a local business or from a state employment agency to come and speak to the class about interviewing. The representative might answer students' questions and then conduct mock interviews. Ask students to have completed job applications for the interviewer to use. After each interview, allow time for the class to discuss the interview or ask questions about it. Before the interviewer's visit, review with the class the important components of an interview: punctuality, neatness in appearance, good eye contact, and good posture. Have students practice what they will say at their interviews. Have students come dressed appropriately on the day the interviewer is to visit. If possible, audio- or video-tape the interviews to help students better assess their interviewing styles. Let students give feedback on the success of their interviews. What were their strengths? How could they make the next interview better?

Unit 10 Overview

UNIT WARM-UP

The focus of Unit 10, "Transportation and Travel," is identifying kinds of transportation, using public transportation, and reading traffic signs. As a warm-up, ask students how they get to school and to work. You may want to bring in pictures of different types of transportation to stimulate conversation.

Unit 10 Optional Materials

● Pictures of different types of transportation being driven by both men and women.

● Pictures of traffic signs and warnings used in traffic control.

● Overhead transparencies and/or realia of public transportation schedules: bus, train, subway, etc.

● Realia of public transportation, tickets, tokens, schedules, and passes.

● Bus route maps, a driver's license, a U.S. road map.

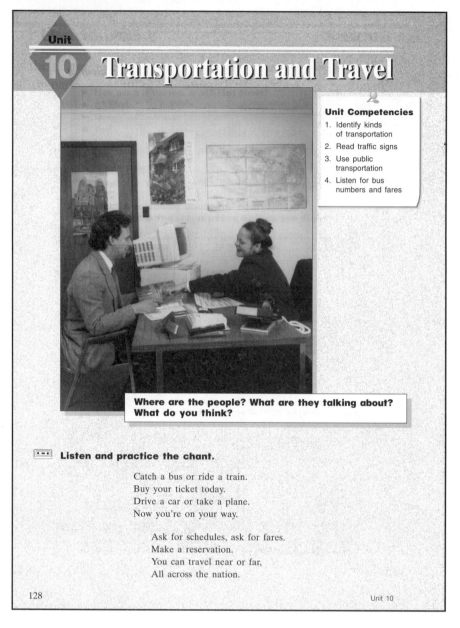

Unit 10

Transportation and Travel

Unit Competencies
1. Identify kinds of transportation
2. Read traffic signs
3. Use public transportation
4. Listen for bus numbers and fares

Where are the people? What are they talking about? What do you think?

Listen and practice the chant.

Catch a bus or ride a train.
Buy your ticket today.
Drive a car or take a plane.
Now you're on your way.

Ask for schedules, ask for fares.
Make a reservation.
You can travel near or far,
All across the nation.

128   Unit 10

COMPETENCIES (page 128)

Identify kinds of transportation

Use public transportation

PREPARATION

Use pictures and realia to preteach the new language in the chant. Follow these suggestions.

● Hold up pictures of a **bus, train, car,** and **plane.** Say the names and have students repeat.

● Hold up realia of ticket, schedules, fares. Say the names and have students repeat. Explain that a fare is the money you pay for a trip on public transportation. Have students repeat. You may also want to present **reservation,** as in making an airplane reservation.

PRESENTATION

Focus attention on the photo and have students answer the questions. Encourage them to say everything they can about it. Write their ideas on the board or restate them in acceptable English.

Present the chant. See "Presenting Chants" on page vi.

WORKBOOK

Unit 10, Page 73, Exercise 1.

FOLLOW-UP

How Do You Get to School? Have students work in small groups to list the different types of transportation they take. Have groups report to the class and create a combined list.

♦ Have students write one or two paragraphs about the methods of transportation they use to get to school or work. Have volunteers share their work with the class.

Starting Out

 A. Look and read.

➤ How do you get to work?
● We always take the bus.
The fare's $1.50.

➤ How do you get to work?
● I'm in a car pool.
We take turns driving.

➤ How does he get to work?
● He usually takes the subway.
A token is $1.75.

➤ How do they get to work?
● They always walk.
They never drive.

B. Answer the questions.

1. Where are the people going? How do they get there?
2. How do you get to school? How do you get to work?

Unit 10   129

PREPARATION

Use the pictures you used with page 128 to preteach the new language. Follow this suggestion.

● Use pictures and realia to present **car pool, subway, fare,** and **token.** Say the names and have students repeat.

Teaching Note: You may want to explain to students that many people take car pools to work. In many car pools, members take turns driving on a daily or a weekly basis. In other car pools, one person always drives and the riders pay the driver.

PRESENTATION

A. Have students talk about the photographs. Encourage them to say everything they can about them. Write their ideas on the board or restate them in acceptable English. Then present the dialogs. See "Presenting Dialogs" on page vi.

B. Demonstrate by doing part of item one on the board. Have students complete the activity independently. Ask several students to read their answers aloud while the other students check their own answers.

WORKBOOK

Unit 10, Page 73, Exercise 2.

FOLLOW-UP

Rules of the Road: Have students work in small groups to discuss the unspoken rules of etiquette and safety on public transportation. They could consider such questions as, Should you give your seat to an older adult? To a mother and child? Do you talk to the driver? How do you request the driver to stop and let you exit? Do you have to use a certain door to exit? Have the groups report their conversations to the class.

♦ Have students write and illustrate the points of etiquette and safety they discussed in their groups on posters. Display the posters in the classroom.

COMPETENCIES (page 130)
Identify kinds of transportation
Listen for bus numbers and fares

Talk It Over

A. Practice the dialogs.

➤ Excuse me.
   Which bus goes to **Elm Street?**
● Bus **25.**
➤ Thanks.

➤ Excuse me.
   Does this bus go to **Elm Street?**
● **Yes, it does.**

 **B. Work with a partner. Where do you want to go?
Use the dialogs in A to find the bus you need.**

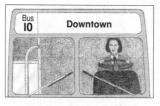
Bus 10 — Downtown

Bus 38 — Parkview Mall

Bus 42 — City Community College

Bus 14 — Train Station

130

Unit 10

PREPARATION

You may want to review the vocabulary for this unit. Follow this suggestion.

● Use the pictures and realia you used with page 128 to review **bus.** Say the name and have students repeat.

PRESENTATION

A. Have students look at the pictures. Encourage them to say everything they can about them. Write their ideas on the board or restate them in acceptable English. Then present the dialog. See "Presenting Dialogs" on page vi.

B. Demonstrate with a student by using the dialog in A to talk about a place you want to go. Have students complete the activity. Ask several students to present their dialogs to the class.

WORKBOOK

Unit 10, Page 74, Exercise 3.

FOLLOW-UP

Public Transportation Fares: Have students work in small groups. Have each group choose a form of local transportation (such as bus, train, subway, or taxi) and find out the fares from your school to different destinations such as a mall or a hospital. Have them find out if fares are higher at certain times of the day or on certain routes, how much trans- fers cost, if using tokens or buying a monthly pass is cheaper than paying cash, etc. Have each group use the same destinations so groups can easily compare their information. Have each group report their findings to the class.

♦ Using the information on fares from the previous activity, have a class discussion comparing different forms of public transportation. Have students discuss which form is most economical, which form is most time efficient, and which form is most easily accessible.

Identify kinds of transportation
Read traffic signs

Word Bank

A. Study the vocabulary.

		Traffic Signs and Signals	
bicycle	fare	bus stop	one way
bus	station	do not enter	speed limit
car	token	don't walk	stop
subway		hospital	walk
train		no parking	yield
car pool		no U-turn	
driver's license			

The red light means stop.
The yellow light means drive
 with caution or slow down.
The green light means go.

B. What are they? Write the words from A.

1. _____train_____   2. _____bicycle_____

3. _____car_____   4. _____subway_____

 C. Work with a small group.
 Talk about how you get to the supermarket and to school.

Unit 10   131

PREPARATION

Preteach or review the new vocabulary before students open their books. Use the pictures and realia you used with page 128. Give special attention to **bicycle, driver's license,** and **station.** To present traffic signs and signals, display the traffic signs and give their meanings.

PRESENTATION

A. Have students scan the list. Define, or have students define, any words individuals do not recognize. Provide any reinforcement necessary. See "Reinforcing Vocabulary" on page vi. Remind students that they can use this list throughout the unit to look up words, to check spelling, and to find key phrases.

B. Demonstrate by writing the first answer on the board. Have students complete the activity independently. Have several students read their answers aloud while other students check their own answers.

C. Have students work in small groups. Have students use the words in A to talk about how they get to the supermarket and to school. Have several groups repeat their conversations for the class.

WORKBOOK

Unit 10, Pages 74–75, Exercises 4A–4C.

FOLLOW-UP

Driving in America: Have students work in small groups to discuss how to get a driver's license. Have the groups summarize their information and share it with the class.

♦ Have the groups from the previous activity write the main points of how to get a driver's license on charts. Display the charts in the classroom.

Listening

 A. Look and listen. Write the bus number on the bus.

Listen again. Match the destination to the correct bus. Write the letter on the bus.

a. Park Street
b. Downtown
✔ c. Mall

Listen again. Write the fares on the signs.

FARE
$ _____1.00_____

FARE
$ _____1.75_____

FARE
$ _____1.50_____

 B. Work with a partner. Follow the dialog. Talk about the buses in A.

➤ Which bus goes to **the mall?**
● Bus **8.**
➤ How much is the fare?
● **$1.00.**

132   Unit 10

PREPARATION

If necessary, review **bus** and **fare.** Use the pictures and realia you used with page 128. Provide any reinforcement necessary. See "Reinforcing Vocabulary" on page vi.

PRESENTATION

A. Have students read the directions for the first part of the activity. Make sure students understand that they will listen and fill in the correct number on the vehicle. Have students listen and complete the first part of the activity as you play the tape or read the Listening Transcript aloud two or more times. Repeat the same procedure with the remaining parts of A. Check students' work.

B. Demonstrate by modeling the activity with a student. Have students work in pairs to complete the activity. Invite several pairs of students to share their dialogs with the class.

WORKBOOK

Unit 10, Page 76, Exercise 5.

FOLLOW-UP

Which Bus Do I Take? Have students work in pairs. Pass out copies of local bus route maps. Have students read the maps, trace the bus routes, and give bus numbers. Have volunteers show the routes they use the most (or would most likely use) to the class.

♦ Have pairs of students take the roles of bus driver and passenger. Have them use the bus route map to create conversations in which travelers ask questions about destinations and bus numbers. Have volunteers repeat their conversations for the class.

Reading

A. Look at the bus route map and the schedule. Where can you go on Bus 20?

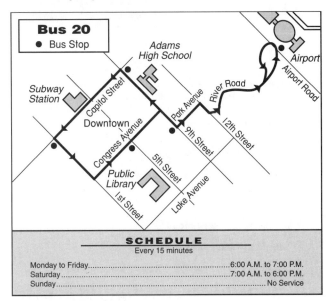

Bus 20
● Bus Stop

SCHEDULE
Every 15 minutes

Monday to Friday...6:00 A.M. to 7:00 P.M.
Saturday ....7:00 A.M. to 6:00 P.M.
Sunday .... No Service

B. Read the sentences.
Use the map and the schedule in A.
Are the sentences true or false? Write _T_ or _F_.

_T_ 1. Bus 20 runs from downtown to the airport.

_F_ 2. You can catch Bus 20 at 5th Street and Lake Avenue.

_T_ 3. Bus 20 stops at Airport and River Road.

_F_ 4. You can take Bus 20 to the airport on Sunday.

 C. Work with a partner.
Talk about the map and the schedule in A.
Where do you want to go?
Where and when can you catch the bus?

COMPETENCIES (page 133)
Use public transportation
Listen for bus numbers and fares

PREPARATION

Use realia or an overhead transparency of a bus schedule and demonstrate how to read it.

Teaching Note: You might explain that transfers are used when a passenger needs to take more than one bus to get to a destination. Remind students that transfers must be asked for when paying the fare.

PRESENTATION

A. Have students look at the map and schedule. Encourage them to say everything they can about them. Write their ideas on the board or restate them in acceptable English. Then have them answer the question.

B. Have students look at the map and schedule and complete the activity independently. Check students' work.

C. Demonstrate by using the map and schedule to talk about a place on the map you would like to go. Have students work with partners. Have students complete the activity. Have several pairs share their answers with the class.

WORKBOOK

Unit 10, Page 77, Exercise 6.

FOLLOW-UP

Cost of Transportation: Have students work in small groups with members who take public transportation and members who drive to school. Have students compare the cost of each type of transportation. Have them discuss the advantages and disadvantages of each type of transportation, also. Have the groups share their conclusions with the class.

♦ Have groups of students compile the information from the previous activity into a poster or chart. Have them compare the relative costs as well as the advantages and disadvantages of each type of transportation. Display the posters or charts in the classroom.

Structure Base

A. Study the examples.

always	100%
usually	
sometimes	
never	0%

I always go to the park on Sunday.

B. Work with a partner.
Use the words in A to talk about what you do.

C. Study the examples.

I always go to the bank on Friday.

I'm going to the bank right now.

D. Complete the sentences.
Write the correct form of the word.
Follow the examples in C.

1. I usually ____take____ **(take)** the bus to school.

2. Right now I'm ____waiting____ **(wait)** for the bus.

3. Sometimes my sister ____drives____ **(drive)** to school.

4. I never ____walk____ **(walk)** to school.

5. I always ____arrive____ **(arrive)** at school on time.

134   Unit 10

PREPARATION

If necessary, review the vocabulary in the language boxes with students before they open their books. Follow the instructions in "Preparation" on page 128.

PRESENTATION

A. Have students read the language boxes independently. Have students use the words in the boxes to say as many sentences as they can. Explain to students that they can refer to the language boxes throughout the unit to check or review sentence patterns.

B. Demonstrate by modeling the activity with a student. Then have students work in pairs to complete the activity. Have several students share their conversations with the class.

C. Follow the procedure in A.

D. Demonstrate by writing the first item on the board. Have students complete the activity independently. Have several students read their completed sentences aloud while the other students check their own answers.

E. Study the example.

> Which bus do I take?

F. Read the bus signs.
Write the questions.
Follow the example in E.

6   City Park

8   Baytown Mall

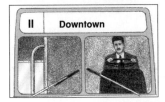
11   Downtown

38   Airport

➤ Which bus do I take to City Park?
● Bus 6.

➤ Which bus do I take to the airport?
● Bus 38.

➤ Which bus do I take to Baytown Mall?
● Bus 8.

➤ Which bus do I take downtown?
● Bus 11.

G. Work with a partner.
Ask each other about transportation where you live.
Follow the examples in F.

PRESENTATION

E. Follow the procedure in A.

F. Demonstrate by modeling the activity with a student. Have students complete the activity independently. Then invite several students to share their questions with the class.

G. Demonstrate by having a student ask you about transportation you take. Have students work in pairs to complete the activity. Have several pairs of students share their conversations with the class.

WORKBOOK

Unit 10, Pages 78–79, Exercises 7A–7C.

FOLLOW-UP

Planning the Day: Distribute bus route maps to small groups of students. Have students use the maps to plan a busy day of errands. Have students write a list of places they want to go. Then have them use the maps to plan their routes to get their errands done efficiently. Have several pairs of students share their routes with the class.

♦ Distribute U.S. road maps to small groups of students. Have students use the maps to plan cross-country trips to places they'd like to visit. Have them decide what modes of transportation to take. Have volunteers share their trip plans with the class.

COMPETENCIES (page 136)
Use public transportation
Listen for bus numbers and fares

Write It Down

**A. Linh lives near Daniel.
She wants to know how to get to City Adult School.
Look at Daniel's map. Complete the directions.**

Central	Freedom	left	State

1. Catch Bus 42 at _____State_____ Street
   and Freedom Road.

2. Get off at _____Freedom_____ Road
   and Central Avenue.

3. Walk one block north on _____Central_____ Avenue.

4. City Adult School is on the _____left_____ .

About You

**B. How do you get from home to school?
Draw a map on a sheet of paper.
Write directions for the way you usually travel.**

136

Unit 10

PREPARATION

If necessary, review **bus** and map directions. Draw a compass on the board and point out **North, South, East,** and **West.** Say the names and have students repeat.

PRESENTATION

A. Have students look at the map. Encourage them to say everything they can about it. Write their ideas on the board or restate them in acceptable English. Have students complete the activity independently. Have several students read their answers aloud while other students check their own answers.

About You
B. Have students work in pairs. Have students read the directions and complete the activity.

Check students' work. Have volunteers share their maps with the class.

WORKBOOK
Unit 10, Page 79, Exercise 8.

FOLLOW-UP

Mapping a Bus Route: Distribute bus route maps to pairs of students. Have each student use the map to give directions from school to their own homes (or any other destination they choose). The students should tell what buses to take and where to catch the buses. Have the partner listen to the directions and draw the route. Have partners compare maps to check for accuracy. Have volunteers share their maps with the class.

♦ Have students write directions that go with the maps their partners drew in the previous activity. Have volunteers share their maps and directions with the class and compare the maps with the written directions. Post the maps and written directions on a bulletin board.

One To One

Student A

Use public transportation

Listen for bus numbers and fares

**1. A customer is at City Transportation Office.
Practice the dialog.**

➤ I want to go to **Central Elementary School.** Which bus do I take?

● **32.**

➤ Where do I catch the bus?

● At **Market Street and Front Street.**

 **2. You're at City Transportation Office.
Ask Student B about the bus routes to these places.
Follow the dialog in 1. Write the information.**

a. Central Elementary School:

Bus ___32___ at Market Street and _____Front_____ Street

b. City Library:

Bus ___32___ at _____Market_____ Street and Front Street

c. Train Station:

Bus ___47___ at Market Street and _____Main_____ Street

 **3. You work at City Transportation Office.
Student B wants to know about bus routes.
Use the bus route map. Follow the dialog in 1.**

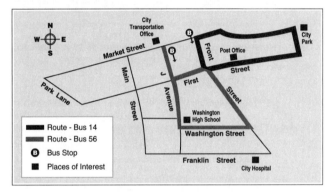

PREPARATION

If necessary, review the language used for asking directions. Use the dialogs on page 130.

PRESENTATION

Teaching Note: For more information on these pages, see "One to One" on page vii.

1. Have students find partners. Assign the roles of A and B. Explain that Student A looks only at page A (page 137) and Student B looks only at page B (page 138). Have them turn to the appropriate pages. Then present the dialog. See "Presenting Dialogs" on page vi.

2. Have students read the directions independently.

Model the activity with a student. Then have students complete the activity.

3. Have students look at the map and locate the streets. Have students read the directions and complete the activity. Then have students switch roles (A becomes B and B becomes A) and repeat steps 2 and 3.

WORKBOOK

Unit 10, Page 80, Exercise 9.

FOLLOW-UP

Giving Directions: Pass out local bus route maps to pairs of students. Have one student use the map to give directions to the other student to

places of local interest. Directions should have the school as the point of origin. Have students switch roles and repeat the activity. Have volunteers share their conversations with the class.

♦ Using the information in the previous activity, have students write the directions for their partners. Have the partners check the directions against the route maps. Ask volunteers to share their directions with the class.

Use public transportation

Listen for bus numbers and fares

One To One Student B

**1. A customer is at City Transportation Office.
Practice the dialog.**

➤ I want to go to **Central Elementary School.** Which bus do I take?
● **32.**
➤ Where do I catch the bus?
● At **Market Street and Front Street.**

**2. You're at City Transportation Office.
Student A wants to know about bus routes.
Use the bus route map. Follow the dialog in 1.**

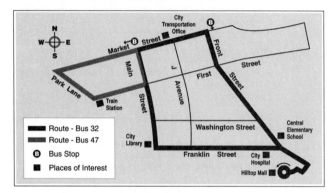

**3. You're at City Transportation Office.
Ask Student A about the bus routes to these places.
Follow the dialog in 1. Write the information.**

a. Washington High School:

Bus ___56___ at Market Street and ___J___ Avenue

b. City Park:

Bus ___14___ at ___Market___ Street and Front Street

c. Post Office:

Bus ___14___ at ___Market___ Street and Front Street

PRESENTATION

Follow the instructions on page 137.

Extension

A. Look at the traffic signs.

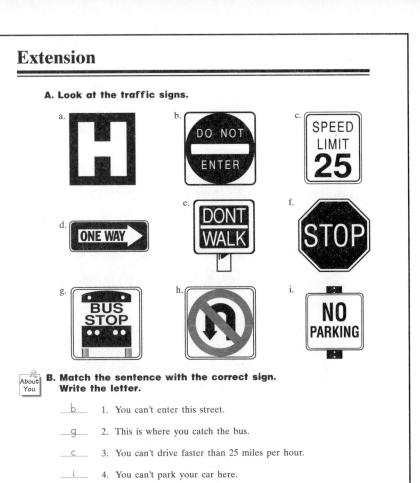

B. Match the sentence with the correct sign. Write the letter.

  b   1. You can't enter this street.

  g   2. This is where you catch the bus.

  c   3. You can't drive faster than 25 miles per hour.

  i   4. You can't park your car here.

  d   5. Cars can go in one direction only on this street.

  e   6. Don't cross the street now.

  a   7. There's a hospital near here.

  f   8. You have to stop completely here.

  h   9. You can't turn around here.

Unit 10   139

PREPARATION

If necessary, review the traffic signs. Follow the instructions in "Preparation" on page 131.

PRESENTATION

A. Have students read the directions. Have students read the signs and discuss where they might be seen. Write their ideas on the board or restate them in acceptable English.

B. Demonstrate by doing the first item on the board. Have students work independently to complete the activity in writing. Have several students say their answers aloud while other students check their own answers.

WORKBOOK

Unit 10, Page 80, Exercise 10.

FOLLOW-UP

Signs in the City: Draw a simple map of several city blocks on the board or on a large piece of paper. Have students make suggestions about what buildings to put on the map (schools, stores, homes, hospital, etc.). Add their suggestions to the map. Then have the class decide where in the city to put safety signs and traffic lights. Have students place the signs on the map in appropriate areas **(Speed Limit 25** in front of a school). Encourage discussion about where to put the signs and why students think they should go in these places.

♦ Have students write the traffic rules that apply to the signs in the previous activities. Have them write the reason for the sign and what drivers or pedestrians are supposed to do. For example, a **Speed Limit 25** sign in front of a school would be there so people drive slowly when children are present. Drivers are expected to slow down to 25 miles per hour or less. Have volunteers share their traffic rules with the class.

Check Your Competency

Unit 10

Can you use the competencies?

- ☐ 1. Identify kinds of transportation
- ☐ 2. Read traffic signs
- ☐ 3. Use public transportation
- ☐ 4. Listen for bus numbers and fares

 A. Use competency I. Complete the sentences.

| bus   subway   car pool   walk |

1. They take the _subway_ to work.   2. They take the _bus_ to school.

3. They're in a _car pool_.   4. They _walk_ to work.

PRESENTATION

Use any of the procedures in "Evaluation," page viii, with these pages. For exercise D, play the tape or read the Listening Transcript aloud two or more times. Record individuals' results on the Unit 10 Individual Competency Chart. Record the class's results on the Class Cumulative Competency Chart.

B. Use competency 2. Talk about the traffic signs.
What do you do? What don't you do?

C. Review competency 3.
Sandra is asking for directions.
Read the bus sign. Complete the dialog.

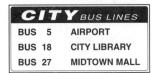

CITY *BUS LINES*

BUS 5	AIRPORT
BUS 18	CITY LIBRARY
BUS 27	MIDTOWN MALL

➤ I want to go to **City Library.** Which _____bus_____ do I take?

● Take bus ____18____.

 Use competency 3. Look at the bus sign.
You're at the City Transportation Office.
Where do you want to go?
Use the dialog above to ask about bus routes.

 D. Use competency 4. Write the bus numbers in column A.

	A	B
1.	25	$1.00
2.	7	$1.75
3.	16	$1.00

Listen again. Write the fares in column B.

Unit 10   141

FOLLOW-UP

ENGLISH IN ACTION

An Optional Cooperative Learning Project: A Local Transportation Guide. You might want students to work together to compile a Class Transportation Guide. Have students work in small groups. Each group can research a form of local transportation, such as taxi companies, bus service, subway and train service, etc. Groups can collect information on schedules, routes, and fares.

If there are a limited number of local transportation possibilities, have students investigate different forms of nationwide travel, such as airlines, long distance bus companies, and trains. You may want to divide the Transportation Guide into local and long distance sections.

Groups can summarize their findings in writing and then combine all the summaries in a Transportation Guide. Reproduce the Transportation Guide for class members, or put it into a binder for students to use in the classroom. Provide time for students to discuss the research process, the information they discovered, and how it will be helpful to them in the future.

Listening Transcript

Unit 1

Listening (Page 6)
Exercise A.
Look, listen, and complete the name.

1. A: What's your first name?
   B: Mei.
   A: How do you spell that?
   B: M-E-I.
   A: Is that M-E-I?
   B: Yes. That's right.
2. A: Ana, what's your last name?
   B: Smith. S-M-I-T-H.
   A: Could you repeat that?
   B: S-M-I-T-H. Smith.
   A: Thanks, Ana.
3. A: Hi. I'm Carlos.
   B: What?
   A: Carlos. C-A-R-L-O-S.
   B: What?
   A: C-A-R-L-O-S.
   B: Oh, Carlos. Good to meet you.
4. A: What's your name?
   B: Pablo.
   A: Could you spell that, please?
   B: Sure. P-A-B-L-O.
   A: Is that P-A-B-L-O?
   B: Yes, it is.
   A: Thanks.

Exercise B.
Look, listen, and write the area code.

1. A: Sabrina, I need you to look up some area codes for me.
   B: OK, Tim. What cities?
   A: Chicago.
   B: Chicago is 312.
   A: What did you say?
   B: 312.
2. A: OK. New York City.
   B: That's 212.
   A: Right. 212. I should know that. That's my mother's area code.
3. A: Now Miami.
   B: 305.
   A: Is that 305?
   B: Yes.
4. A: OK. Washington, D.C.
   B: 202. Did you get that?

A: Yeah. 202. Thanks.
B: Is that all?
A: Yes. Thanks for your help.

Exercise C.
Look, listen, and write the number.

1. A: So your city and state are Chicago, Illinois. What's your ZIP Code?
   B: 60657.
   A: Is that 60657?
   B: Yes. It is.
2. A: Your area code?
   B: 312.
3. A: And your phone number?
   B: 555-0857.
   A: So that's 555-0857?
   B: Yes.
4. A: Do you have a Social Security number?
   B: Yes. It's 345-54-9822.
   A: Could you repeat that?
   B: Yes. It's 345-54-9822.
   A: Thanks, Mr. Rizzo. Here's your identification card.
   B: Thanks a lot.

Exercise D.
Look, listen, and complete the form.

A: Your name, please.
B: Elena Martinka.
A: How do you spell that?
B: My first name is Elena. E-L-E-N-A. My last name is Martinka. M-A-R-T-I-N-K-A.
A: That's E-L-E-N-A M-A-R-T-I-N-K-A?
B: Right.
A: Your address, Ms. Martinka?
B: 3440 Lake Street.
A: 3440 L-A-K-E S-T-R-E-E-T?
B: That's right.
A: What's your apartment number?
B: 202.
A: 202. Your city and state?
B: Miami, Florida.
A: M-I-A-M-I F-L-O-R-I-D-A. The ZIP Code?
B: 33153.
A: 33153. Your phone number, area code first.
B: (305) 555-1987.
A: That's (305) 555-1987?
B: Yes.

A: What language do you speak?

B: Russian.

A: And your Social Security number?

B: 281-39-1011.

A: 281-39-1011. Thanks, Ms. Martinka. Welcome to English class.

B: Thanks.

Unit 2

Listening (Page 20)
Exercise A.
Look, listen, and write the places on the map.

1. A: Excuse me. Where's the post office?
   B: It's next to the police station.
   A: Where?
   B: Next to the police station. The post office is on the corner of Main Street and Second Avenue.
   A: On the corner of Main Street and Second Avenue. OK. Thanks.
2. A: Excuse me. Where's the bank?
   B: Across from the supermarket.
   A: Where?
   B: Across from the supermarket, on First Avenue.
   A: Oh, on First Avenue. Is it across from the drug store, too?
   B: Yes. The bank is on the corner of First Avenue and State Street, across from the supermarket and the drug store.
   A: OK. Thanks.
3. A: I'm going to the store.
   B: What store?
   A: The store on Second Avenue.
   B: Next to the laundromat?
   A: Yes. It's between the laundromat and the fire department.
   B: Oh, yes. The store across from the park, right?
   A: Right. Do you want anything?
   B: No, thanks.
4. A: How far is the hospital from here?
   B: One block. It's on Main Street.
   A: On Main Street? Where?
   B: The hospital is on the right, across from the fire department.
   A: On the right, across from the fire

department. Thank you!

Exercise B.
Look, listen, and follow the directions. Draw a line on the map.

A: Excuse me. Where's the movie theater?

B: It's not very far. Walk north on First Avenue. Go one block.

A: Walk one block north?

B: Yes. Then, turn right on State Street. Go one block east to Second Avenue.

A: One block east to Second Avenue. OK.

B: The movie theater is on the corner, across from the supermarket.

A: OK. Thank you.

Check Your Competency (Page 29)
Exercise C.
Use competency 4. Listen to the directions. Draw a line on the map on page 28.

A: Excuse me. Where's the drug store?

B: It's on the corner of Green Street and Oak Street.

A: Where?

B: It's on the corner of Green Street and Oak Street.

A: How do I get there?

B: Go east on Main Street one block.

A: I go east on Main Street one block.

B: Yes. Turn right on Oak Street. Go one block south. The drug store is on the corner of Green Street and Oak Street. It's on the left across the street from the hospital.

A: I turn right on Oak Street and go one block south. It's on the corner of Green Street and Oak Street.

B: That's right. It's on the left across the street from the hospital.

A: On the left across the street from the hospital. Thanks.

Unit 3

Listening (Page 34)
Exercise A.
Look, listen, and write the room numbers.

1. A: Hi. I'm in Level 1 English. Where's my class?

B: Level 1 English is in room 11.

A: Room 11?

B: Yes. Room 11.

A: OK, thanks.

B: You're welcome.

2. A: Excuse me. My name is Lydia Santana. Who's my teacher?

B: What class are you in?

A: I'm in Level 2 English, room 15.

B: Room 15?

A: Yes. 15.

B: Then Mr. Bondar is your teacher.

A: Mr. Bondar?

B: Yes.

A: Thanks for helping me.

B: You're welcome.

3. A: Excuse me. Can you tell me where the Level 3 English class is?

B: It's in room 20.

A: Room 20?

B: Yes. Room 20. Ms. Franklin is your teacher.

A: Ms. Franklin is my teacher?

B: Yes, she is.

A: Thanks. She's a great teacher!

B: You're welcome.

4. A: Excuse me. What's my room number?

B: What class are you in?

A: I'm in Level 4 English.

B: Room 27.

A: Room 27?

B: Yes. Room 27.

A: OK. Thanks for helping me.

B: You're welcome.

Exercise B.
Look, listen, and write the room numbers on the map.

1. A: Where's the director's office?

B: Room 16.

A: Room 16?

B: Yes. Go left here. Then go around the corner and down the hall. Room 16 is on the left.

A: OK. Room 16, on the left. Thanks.

2. A: Excuse me. How do I get to the counselors' office?

B: Turn right. Then go left down the hall. It's next to the computer room.

A: Oh. Is it room 19?

B: Yes. The counselors' office is room 19.

A: Room 19. OK. Thanks.

3. A: Hi, Albert. Where are you going?

B: To the cafeteria.

A: Where's the cafeteria?

B: Next to the exit.

A: What room is it in?

B: The cafeteria's in room 17.

Exercise C.
Look, listen, and follow the directions.
Draw a line on the map.

A: Excuse me. Where's the library?

B: Go left here. Go around the corner and down the hall. Then turn right. The library is on the left.

A: Where?

B: Turn left and then go around the corner and down the hall. Turn right. Then the library is on the left.

A: Turn left. Go around the corner and down the hall. Turn right and it's on my left?

B: Yes. That's where the library is.

A: OK. Thanks.

Check Your Competency (Page 42)
Exercise A.

Use competency 1. Listen. Write the room numbers on the building directory.

1. A: Hi. Can you tell me where the counselors' office is?

B: It's in room 117, I think.

A: Room 117?

B: Right.

A: OK. Thanks.

B: You're welcome.

2. A: Excuse me. What room is the Level 1 English class in?

B: That's room 112.

A: Room 112?

B: Yes, 112. Do you know how to find it?

A: Yes. Thank you.

B: You're welcome.

3. A: Do you know where the library is?

B: The library? It's in room 119.

A: Library...room 119. Thanks.

B: You're welcome.

4. A: Hi. Where can I find the secretary?

B: The secretary's office is room 116.

A: Is that 116?
B: Right, 116.
A: OK. Thanks a lot.
B: You're welcome.

Unit 4

Listening (Page 48)
Exercise A.
Look, listen, and write the time.

1. A: I'm so sleepy this morning. What time is it?
   B: Um. Let me look. It's 9:00.
   A: 9:00! Oh no! I'm late! I have to meet my sister. Bye!
   B: See you later.
2. A: Hey, Joel, what time is your break?
   B: It's 10:45.
   A: Excuse me? 10:45?
   B: Yes.
3. A: When's your lunch break?
   B: 12:15. Would you like to go to lunch today?
   A: Yes. I'll meet you at 12:15, OK?
   B: OK. See you then.
4. A: I go home at 5:30 today.
   B: 5:30?
   A: Yes, 5:30. Can you pick me up?
   B: OK. Where?
   A: I'll be near the stairs.
   B: OK. See you then.

Exercise B.
Look, listen, and circle the date.

1. A: Excuse me. What's today's date?
   B: Monday, June 7.
   A: Excuse me?
   B: Monday, June 7.
   A: Thanks.
2. A: What day do you start school, Lily?
   B: Wednesday.
   A: What's the date Wednesday?
   B: October 26.
   A: Excuse me? Is that October 26?
   B: Yes, the twenty-sixth.
3. A: When's your birthday, Carlos?
   B: It's April 19.
   A: Excuse me? April 19?

B: Yes, April 19.
A: Hey, that's my birthday, too!

Exercise C.
Look and listen to the weather forecast. Write the number of the forecast on the line.

1. Good morning. This is the morning news. It's Saturday, the 4th of July. From New York to California, everyone is celebrating Independence Day. They are swimming, fishing, and going to the beach. The weather forecast: hot and sunny all day today.

2. Welcome to the Weather Break. It's Monday, April 7th. Today's weather will be cool and rainy. The rain and cool weather are expected to continue for the next two or three days.

Check Your Competency (Page 57)
Exercise D.
Use competencies 4 and 5. Listen to the radio weather report. Circle the time, the date, and the weather.

Good morning, everyone. You're listening to Radio WRLE, everyone's favorite radio station. The time is 8:30 on June 14. It's a beautiful Saturday morning. Here's the weather: It's warm and sunny. It will stay warm and sunny all day. It's a beautiful day to go to the park. And now here's the 8:30 news for Saturday, June 14.

Unit 5

Listening (Page 62)
Exercise A.
What are the people looking for? Look, listen, and circle the letter in column A.

1. A: Excuse me. Where can I find the rice?
   B: Let's see. Rice is on aisle 3.
   A: Aisle 3?
   B: Right.
   A: Thanks.
2. A: Excuse me.
   B: Yes. Can I help you?
   A: Yes, thanks. I'm looking for a bottle of cooking oil.
   B: Cooking oil? That's on aisle 5.

B: Cooking oil? That's on aisle 5.

A: Where?

B: Aisle 5.

A: Thank you.

B: You're welcome.

3. A: Where are the carrots?

B: Excuse me?

A: The carrots?

B: Umm, they're in the fruit and vegetable section, aisle 2.

A: Aisle 2?

B: That's right.

A: Thanks.

Listen again and write the aisle number in column B. *[Play the tape or read the transcript of Exercise A aloud again.]*

Exercise B.
Look, listen, and circle the food the people want to buy.

A: Don't forget. Lee and Bo are coming to dinner tonight.

B: That's right. What should we cook?

A: What about hamburgers and French fries? That's my favorite. Bo's too, I think.

B: Good idea. We probably need to make a shopping list.

A: OK. We need two pounds of ground beef.

B: Two pounds?

A: Yes. And we also need some potatoes.

B: How many?

A: Five should be enough.

B: What else?

A: Lettuce and tomatoes.

B: Lettuce and tomatoes.

A: OK. Here's the list: two pounds of ground beef, five potatoes, lettuce, and tomatoes. Is that right?

B: What about a cake?

A: Great idea!

Exercise C.
Listen. Look at the food you circled in B.
Check off the groceries they bought.
Then answer the questions.

A: Let's unpack these groceries, Francisco.

B: OK. Did we get everything?

A: Let's check the shopping list.

B: We have two pounds of ground beef?

A: Yes. Two pounds of ground beef and five potatoes.

B: Five potatoes and the lettuce and tomatoes...

A: Hey, what's this candy doing in here?

B: Candy, great! I'm hungry!

A: Wait a minute. Candy wasn't on the list. Why did you get it?

B: I just wanted some.... Oh, no, guess what! We forgot something!

A: Well, Francisco, you forgot the cake, so you'll just have to go back to the store and get one! And get some apples and oranges, too.

Check Your Competency (Page 71)
Exercise D.
Use competency 5. Look and listen.
Write the aisle numbers.

1. A: Excuse me. I need some rice. Where can I find that?

   B: Rice's on aisle 2.

   A: Where?

   B: Aisle 2.

   A: All right. Thank you.

2. A: Excuse me. Where are the cookies?

   B: Let's see. That'd be aisle 6.

   A: Excuse me?

   B: Cookies are on aisle 6.

   A: Aisle 6. Thanks.

3. A: Where can I find the cooking oil?

   B: Cooking oil would be on aisle 3.

   A: Aisle 3. OK, thanks.

   B: You're welcome.

4. A: Where can I find eggs?

   B: Aisle 1.

   A: Aisle 1. Good. Thank you.

   B: OK. Happy shopping!

Unit 6

Listening (Page 76)
Exercise A.
Look, listen, and circle the letter of the correct tag.

1. A: Excuse me. I need some help.
   B: Yes. How can I help you?
   A: I'm interested in that blouse.
   B: The blue one?
   A: Yes, that one. How much is it?
   B: $10.00.
   A: $10.00...OK. Is there a medium?
   B: Yes. Here's a medium.
   A: May I try it on?
   B: Of course. The dressing room is over there.

2. A: Can I help you?
   B: Yes. I want some white socks.
   A: How many pairs do you want?
   B: I want several pairs of white socks.
   A: We have these packages of six pairs.
   B: I like those. How much are they?
   A: A package of six pairs is $9.99.
   B: How much?
   A: $9.99.
   B: What a bargain! I'll take one package.

3. A: Excuse me. I'm looking for a sweater.
   B: What size do you wear?
   A: Well, I'm very tall and hard to fit.
   B: You probably take an extra-large, then.
   A: How much is an extra-large?
   B: This extra-large sweater's only $24.00.
   A: How much?
   B: $24.00.
   A: I need to try it on first. Where's the dressing room?
   B: The dressing room is around the corner, on your right.
   A: Thanks.

Exercise B.
What are the people buying? Look, listen, and number the pictures in column A.

1. A: Oh, look at those sneakers. I want those for summer.
   B: They *are* cute. How much are they?
   A: $10.00.

B: $10.00? That's not bad. But that other pair is only $8.00.
   A: Yes. But I like these sneakers. They're my size, too. I think I'll spend the $10.00.
   B: Well, here's a cashier.
   C: Hi. Will that be all?
   A: Yes.
   C: How are you paying?
   A: By check.

2. A: Did you say you wanted a T-shirt?
   B: Yes, I did.
   A: The T-shirts on this rack are on sale.
   B: How much are they?
   A: $5.00.
   B: How much?
   A: Only $5.00.
   B: Hey, great. I'd like that blue one.
   A: OK. Do you want to try it on?
   B: No, I know I wear a large. I'll take it.
   A: Fine. How are you paying?
   B: Cash.

3. A: Excuse me. I'm looking for a hat. Are those on sale?
   B: No, they're regular price.
   A: Well, how much is that one?
   B: That hat's on sale. It's half off.
   A: How much is it now?
   B: $15.00.
   A: $15.00?
   B: Yes. Do you want that one?
   A: No, thank you. I'll keep looking.

Listen again and write the price in column B. *[Play the tape or read the transcript of Exercise B aloud again.]*

Listen again. Did the people buy the clothes? How did they pay? Circle *cash, check,* or *didn't buy* in column C. *[Play the tape or read the transcript of Exercise B aloud again.]*

Check Your Competency (Page 85)
Exercise C.
Use competency 4. Listen. Circle the prices.

A: How much are these clothes?
B: The pants are $14.40.
A: How much?

B: $14.40.

A: And the gloves?

B: The gloves are $11.00.

A: What about those T-shirts?

B: Those are $6.99.

A: That's $14.40 and $11.00 and $6.99.

B: The total is $34.98, including tax.

A: I'll write you a check. Did you say $34.98?

B: Yes.

Unit 7

Listening (Page 90)
Exercise A.
Look and listen. Some people are at home. Which rooms are they in? Write the room in column A.

1. A: Hi, Patty. What are you doing?
   B: Hi, Alona. I'm just sitting in the living room, watching TV.
   A: Oh. Should I call back later?
   B: No, I can talk now. In fact, would you like to come over? We can watch TV together.
   A: OK. I'll bring the popcorn and be in your living room in ten minutes!

2. A: Kathleen, where are you?
   B: I'm in the bedroom.
   A: What are you doing?
   B: Studying.
   A: Oh, OK. Let me know when you're finished, and we'll go shopping.
   B: OK. How about in a half-hour?

3. A: Ken, where are you?
   B: I'm in the kitchen, cooking dinner.
   A: Great! What are you cooking?
   B: Hamburgers.
   A: Oh, that sounds good!

Listen again. What are the people doing? Circle the answer in column B. [*Play the tape or read the transcript of Exercise A aloud again.*]

Exercise B.
Look, listen, and number the apartments.

1. A: Excuse me. I'm looking for a one-bedroom apartment. Do you have any available?

B: Yes, we do. We have a very nice one-bedroom near the park. It has a living room, a kitchen, and one bathroom. Are you interested?

A: Maybe. How much is the rent?

B: $450 a month.

A: $450, OK. Is there a deposit?

B: Yes. We require a $100 deposit.

A: $100 isn't bad for a deposit. When can I see it?

B: We can go over there right now.

2. A: World Realty. May I help you?
   B: Yes. I'm interested in the three-bedroom apartment you advertised. Could you tell me how many bathrooms it has?
   A: Let's see…. The three-bedroom apartment has two bathrooms. Is that what you're looking for?
   B: It sure is. We need three bedrooms and two bathrooms. The ad says the rent is $750 a month.
   A: Right. It's $750. There's also a $750 deposit.
   B: Another $750 for deposit? Wow, that's a lot!
   A: Well, it's a very nice place. Are you still interested?
   B: Yes, I guess so. I'll come down to your office later today.
   A: That'd be fine. Thanks.

3. A: Hello. I just saw the for-rent sign out front. Can you give me some information on the apartment?
   B: Sure. It's occupied right now, but I can tell you about it.
   A: That'd be fine.
   B: It has two bedrooms and one bathroom. It's got a living room, and an adjoining kitchen.
   A: Sounds good. Is it furnished?
   B: No, it's not.
   A: Well, that's fine. I'm not looking for a furnished place. I have my own furniture. How much is the rent?
   B: It's $575, and there's a $300 deposit.
   A: $575 rent, with a $300 deposit. Well, I'll think about it. Thanks for your time.
   B: You're welcome.

Listen again. Write the rent and the deposit under the apartment. *[Play the tape or read the transcript of Exercise B aloud again.]*

Unit 8

Listening (Page 104)

Exercise A.

Look and listen. Who do the people need to see? Circle the answer.

1. A: Good morning. Dr. Jacob's office.
   B: Hello. I need to make an appointment for my son to see the doctor for a check-up.
   A: OK. Your name and your son's name please?
   B: My name is Jack Woods. My son is David Woods.
   A: All right, Mr. Woods. We have an opening on Wednesday, March 28, at 4:00.
   B: March 28 at 4:00. That's fine.
   A: Good. We'll see you then.
   B: Thank you.

2. A: Good afternoon. Colton Dental Clinic.
   B: Hello. This is Jennifer Long. I need to see the dentist for a check-up.
   A: Well, the dentist can see you on June 2, at 9:15 in the morning. Is that OK?
   B: Did you say June 2?
   A: Yes, June 2.
   B: OK. And what time did you say?
   A: 9:15 in the morning. Can you be here then?
   B: Yes, that's fine.

3. A: Hello. Office of Doctors Brenner, Chen, and Brown.
   B: Hello. This is Bela Buzek. I need to make an appointment with Dr. Brown.
   A: OK. Dr. Brown can see you this Thursday at 3:30. How's that?
   B: Thursday...wait. What's the date that day?
   A: December 13. Is that all right?
   B: Oh, yes. December 13 is fine. Did you say 3:30?
   A: Yes, 3:30 in the afternoon. Please hold a moment, and I'll be back to get some more information.

Exercise B.

Look and listen. Complete the sentences.

1. A: Hello, Mr. Woods. Hi, David.
   B: Hi, Dr. Jacobs.
   C: Hi.
   A: I see you're here for a check-up, David. How do you feel today?
   C: I feel OK.
   B: He feels fine now, but he gets a lot of stomachaches.
   A: Stomachaches? How much candy do you eat?
   C: Well, I always have a candy bar at lunch. And sometimes I have another one after school.
   A: Well, David, I think you need to stop eating so much candy.
   C: Stop eating candy?
   A: That's right. You can have candy once in a while, but you can't eat it all the time. That's why you get stomachaches.
   C: Well, OK.
   B: Don't worry, Dr. Jacobs. I'll make sure he doesn't eat so much candy.

2. A: Hello, Ms. Long. I'm Dr. Kim. You're here for a check-up?
   B: Hello, Dr. Kim. Yes, just a check-up.
   A: OK. No toothaches or other problems lately?
   B: No, none at all.
   A: Well, that's good. OK, open wide.
   B: OK.
   A: OK, Ms. Long, all done. Everything seems fine.
   B: Thank you, Dr. Kim.
   A: Now, I want you to come back in 6 months for another check-up, OK?
   B: OK, thank you. See you in 6 months.

3. A: Hello, Ms. Buzek. It's good to see you again.
   B: Hello, Dr. Brown.
   A: How do you feel?
   B: Well, I feel sick. First I feel hot. Then I feel cold. I feel tired a lot, too. It started a week ago.
   A: It sounds like you have the flu.
   B: The flu? Is that serious?
   A: Not at all. It's very common this time of year.
   B: What should I do?

A: Well, generally the flu has to run its course. But you need to get plenty of sleep and drink water, tea, and juice. You should feel better in another week.

B: Water, tea, and juice?

A: Yes, and lots of sleep.

Listen again. What does the doctor say? Complete the sentences. *[Play the tape or read the transcript of Exercise B aloud again.]*

Check Your Competency (Page 113)
Exercise D.
Use competency 5. Look and listen. What does the doctor say to do? Number the pictures from 1 to 5.

A: Hello, Ms. Mason. I'm Dr. Hansen. How do you feel?

B: Not very well. I feel hot.

A: Yes. I see you have a fever. Any other symptoms?

B: Yes. My head hurts. I have a sore throat, too.

A: I think you have the flu, Ms. Mason. But I'd better give you a check-up to make sure it's the flu and not something else.

B: OK.

A: First, let's take a look at your throat. Say "ah."

B: Ahhh . . .

A: Yes. I see that it must be sore. OK, now I want to listen to your breathing. Please breathe in. OK. Now breathe out.

B: OK. How's that?

A: Well, that doesn't sound too bad. I'm sure it's the flu, though.

B: What can I do for it?

A: You need to drink water, tea, and juice.

B: What?

A: Drink water, tea, and juice. Also, get plenty of sleep.

B: OK. Drinking water, tea, and juice and sleeping. Is that all?

A: Yes. You should feel better in a few days.

B: Thank you, Doctor.

Unit 9

Listening (Page 118)
Exercise A.
Three people are interviewing for jobs. Look and listen. What were their jobs before? Circle the jobs in column A.

1. A: Hello. My name is Sue Weston. Welcome to the job fair.

   B: Hello. I'm Pedro Mendoza. It's nice to meet you. I'm here to look for a job.

   A: What kind of work are you looking for, Mr. Mendoza?

   B: I'm a mechanic. I've been a mechanic for six years.

   A: What kinds of cars can you fix?

   B: All kinds of cars, both American and foreign.

   A: Mr. Mendoza, can you fix buses, too?

   B: Buses? No, I've never worked on a bus, but I'm sure I can learn.

   A: It's not really a problem. There is a bus company that needs a mechanic, but there are also two car shops that need mechanics. Let me give you their job applications.

   B: Great. Thank you.

2. A: Hello, Mr. Miller. I'm Richard Chu. Welcome to Ready Employment Agency. How can I help you?

   B: Good morning, Mr. Chu. I'm looking for a job.

   A: OK. What experience do you have?

   B: I was a cook for ten years.

   A: Ten years. That's a lot of experience. Were you a cook in a large restaurant?

   B: Yes. I've worked in a large hotel restaurant for the last three years.

   A: Well, Mr. Miller, I'm sure I can help you find a job. I know a local hotel that needs a dinner cook. They also need someone to bake cakes. Do you bake?

   B: Yes, but not very well. I don't have any experience baking cakes.

   A: OK. Then let me give you the application for the cook's position and we'll see what happens.

B: Thank you.

3. A: Good morning. I have an appointment to look for a job through the agency. Are you Ms. Santos?

B: Yes. I'm Miriam Santos. What's your name, please?

A: Christine Powell.

B: Oh, yes, Ms. Powell. What kind of job are you looking for?

A: Well, I was a cab driver before. But there's not enough business here. I'd like another job that pays a little more.

B: You can drive a cab. That's good. How about trucks or buses?

A: I can drive a bus. I have a license for that. I can't drive a truck, though.

B: OK. I have an opening for a bus driver. Would you be interested? It's with a very nice company.

A: Yes, I would.

Listen again. What can they do now?
Circle the skills in column B. *[Play the tape or read the transcript of Exercise A aloud again.]*

Exercise B.
Soo-ha Lee is calling about a job. Look and listen. Read the questions. Circle the answers.

A: Green Garden Company. May I help you?

B: Yes. I'm calling about the gardener's job in the newspaper. My name is Soo-ha Lee.

A: Hello, Ms. Lee. My name is Lilia Silverman. I'm going to ask you some questions, get a little information, and then have someone call you back. Is that OK with you?

B: OK.

A: First, please spell your name for me.

B: It's Soo-ha, S-O-O, hyphen, H-A. Lee, L-E-E.

A: Thank you. Now, do you have any experience?

B: Yes. I was a gardener for a company that takes care of gardens for large apartment buildings and houses.

A: Oh, for how long?

B: Three months. It was a summer job. And I have some experience in my own garden, too. I grow a lot of my own plants.

A: Oh, I'll write all that down. Can you take care of trees?

B: Well, I didn't do that at my last job. But I'm sure I can learn.

A: OK, Ms. Lee. The only other thing I need for now is your phone number.

B: It's 555-2133.

A: 555-2133. OK, thank you. Someone will call you soon.

B: Thank you very much.

Unit 10

Listening (Page 132)
Exercise A.
Look and listen. Write the bus number on the bus.

1. A: I want to go to the mall. Which bus do I take?

B: Take number 8.

A: Which bus?

B: 8. It goes to the mall. It's leaving in fifteen minutes.

A: OK. How much is the fare?

B: $1.00.

A: $1.00, OK. Thanks!

B: You're welcome.

2. A: Excuse me. Does this bus go to Park Street?

B: No, it doesn't. Bus 27 goes to Park Street. You can get the 27 across the street.

A: Do you know the fare?

B: $1.75.

A: Does the $1.75 need to be exact change?

B: Yes, it does.

3. A: I'm going downtown. Which bus do I take?

B: Number 45.

A: Excuse me?

B: Bus 45 goes downtown.

A: Oh, OK. Where can I get it?

B: Right here. It should be here in about ten minutes.

A: Great. Do you know if the fare's still $1.50?

B: Yes. From here to downtown is $1.50.

A: $1.50? Thanks for your help.

B: You're welcome.

Listen again. Match the destination to the correct bus. Write the letter on the bus. *[Play the tape or read the transcript of Exercise A aloud again.]*

Listen again. Write the fares on the signs. *[Play the tape or read the transcript of Exercise A aloud again.]*

Check Your Competency (Page 141)
Exercise D.
Use competency 4. Write the bus numbers in column A.

1. A: Excuse me. Does this bus go to City Hospital?

   B: No, it doesn't. You have to take bus 25.

   A: Which bus?

   B: 25.

   A: How much is the fare?

   B: $1.00.

   A: Only $1.00? Great. Thanks.

2. A: I'm going to City Park. Which bus do I take?

   B: Take bus 7.

   A: How much is the fare for bus 7?

   B: $1.75.

   A: Excuse me? How much?

   B: $1.75.

   A: OK, thanks.

3. A: I want to go to City Adult School. Which bus do I take?

   B: Take bus 16.

   A: How much is the fare for bus 16?

   B: $1.00.

   A: The fare's $1.00?

   B: That's right.

   A: Thank you.

Listen again. Write the fares in column B.

[Play the tape or read the transcript of Exercise A aloud again.]

Individual Competency Chart

Student _____

Class _____

Teacher _____

Level 1 ♦ Unit 1

Competencies	Date Presented	Date Checked	Result (✔)	Comments
1. Ask for and give personal information				
2. Say hello				
3. Introduce oneself				
4. Complete an identification form				

Level 1 ♦ Unit 2

Competencies	Date Presented	Date Checked	Result (✔)	Comments
1. Identify places				
2. Tell where places are				
3. Read maps				
4. Ask for, give, and follow directions				
5. Use a pay phone to report an emergency				

Individual Competency Chart

Student _____

Class _____

Teacher _____

Level 1 ♦ Unit 3

Competencies	Date Presented	Date Checked	Result (✔)	Comments
1. Listen for room numbers				
2. Identify people and places at school				
3. Talk about where places are in buildings				
4. Read building directories				
5. Write absentee notes				

Level 1 ♦ Unit 4

Competencies	Date Presented	Date Checked	Result (✔)	Comments
1. Talk about seasons and weather				
2. Ask for, say, and write times and dates				
3. Read calendars				
4. Listen for times and dates				
5. Listen to weather forecasts				
6. Read store hour signs				

Real-Life English

Individual Competency Chart

Student _____

Class _____

Teacher _____

Level 1 ♦ Unit 5

Competencies	Date Presented	Date Checked	Result (✔)	Comments
1. Identify kinds of food				
2. Write shopping lists				
3. Identify food packaging				
4. Ask where things are in a supermarket				
5. Listen for aisle numbers				
6. Read price tags and expiration dates				

Level 1 ♦ Unit 6

Competencies	Date Presented	Date Checked	Result (✔)	Comments
1. Identify clothes by article, size, and color				
2. Shop for clothes				
3. Read clothing ads and comparison shop				
4. Listen for and say prices and totals				
5. Read size tags, price tags, and receipts				
6. Write checks				

Individual Competency Chart

Student _____

Class _____

Teacher _____

Level 1 ♦ Unit 7

Competencies	Date Presented	Date Checked	Result (✔)	Comments
1. Identify rooms, furniture, and kinds of housing				
2. Read for-rent ads				
3. Ask for utilities to be turned on				
4. Ask for simple repairs				

Level 1 ♦ Unit 8

Competencies	Date Presented	Date Checked	Result (✔)	Comments
1. Identify kinds of health clinics				
2. Read a thermometer				
3. Make doctors' appointments				
4. Talk about symptoms and injuries				
5. Listen to doctors' instructions				

Individual Competency Chart

Student _____

Class _____

Teacher _____

Level 1 ♦ Unit 9

Competencies	Date Presented	Date Checked	Result (✔)	Comments
1. Identify kinds of jobs				
2. Give their work experience and skills				
3. Read help-wanted ads				
4. Complete job applications				
5. Understand safety warnings				

Level 1 ♦ Unit 10

Competencies	Date Presented	Date Checked	Result (✔)	Comments
1. Identify kinds of transportation				
2. Read traffic signs				
3. Use public transportation				
4. Listen for bus numbers and fares				

Class Cumulative Competency Chart

Level 1 ◆ Unit _____   Class _____

Teacher _____

Competencies

Name									Comments

Real-Life English